Inquiry into the Nature of Women's Exploitation

Ariane Loening

© Ariane Loening
Published in 2024 by The Bruges Group

ISBN: 978-1-7390920-3-0

The Bruges Group Publications Office
246 Linen Hall, 162-168 Regent Street, London W1B 5TB
www.brugesgroup.com

Bruges Group publications are not intended to represent a corporate view of European and international developments. Contributions are chosen on the basis of their intellectual rigour, and their ability to open up new avenues for debate.

Twitter @brugesgroup, LinkedIn @brugesgroup
GETTR @brugesgroup, Telegram t.me/brugesgroup, Facebook @brugesgroup
Instagram @brugesgroup, YouTube @brugesgroup

Inquiry into the Nature of Women's Exploitation was written when the author lived in West Bengal, had learnt Bengali and developed good contacts with rural organisations through her homeopathic practice and translating work. Having gone to India to try to understand the reasons for poverty and remained in West Bengal because of the people's hospitality, ethics, frankness and passion for education and social improvement, she came to understand some of the deep-rooted cultural and attitudinal aspects of, in particular, rural life, where the poverty was usually worst.

The author collaborated with NGOs involved in maternal and child health and women's income-generation schemes, and was also aware that many income-generating schemes for women did not succeed. It became clear that the lack of time to attend clinics and to make the products for selling was the main factor enforcing many women's personal poverty, dependence, social weakness, ill-health and unhappiness. This led the author to do a time and energy use study of the housework and childcare done by girls and women from many families in the villages of North 24-Parganas District, and to include an account of family members' attitudes to the value of these tasks.

Once the results were collated and the narrative (of what was a complex issue) written, a book called *Sharger Bheet (The Roots of Heaven)* was printed in Bengali and distributed by the author to all the families and organisations who had supported the research. The United Nations, Indian women's organisations at national level and academics had long been investigating women's oppression within the Indian patriarchal system. The author believed it was necessary, first, to pick apart the cultural norm that it had to be girls and women who always did all the family's housework and childcare, and then to challenge the accepted notion that all this work was valueless.

The emotional and physical lives of the girls and women were inquired into and many answers revealed by observation as well as questions relating to what happened before and after marriage, during pregnancy and after the birth of children. Significant social, cultural and biological aspects have been interrogated in order to challenge norms and stimulate changes in perspectives for the better.

Inquiry into the Nature of Women's Exploitation was written in order to assemble ideas about the psychological, historical and contemporary reasons for the gross differences in life opportunities and experiences of men and women in rural West Bengal and beyond. As a result of her inquiry, the author came to a couple of conclusions concerning time management in the home and men and women's differing reproductive consciousness; an awareness that is essential for us all to create a fair and peaceful society wherever we live. And - to curtail unjustly won male privilege, men's assumptions of entitlement, misogyny, rape and war-mongering - psychological perspectives must change in order to promote and reward men's bravery, innate protectiveness, artistic genius and strength. This change will only happen when the essential labour needed inside and outside the home to maintain and reproduce life is shared, appreciated and valued properly.

Table of Contents

ACKNOWLEDGEMENTS 1

ABOUT MYSELF 3

PREFACE 4

WHY DISCUSS HOUSEWORK, REPRODUCTION AND CHILDCARE? 5

BACKGROUND TO THE SURVEY 7

ORIGINAL MANUSCRIPT 8

HOUSEHOLDS SURVEYED 9

FINDINGS OF THE SURVEY 10
   A. HOUSEWORK 10
   B. REPRODUCTION AND CHILDCARE 31

SUBVERSION, FEMINISM AND AWARENESS 41

REPRODUCTION (from sexual intercourse to the child) 44

MARRIAGE 46

IMAGES OF VILLAGE WOMEN 48

THE INVISIBLE REALITY OF WOMEN (India and West Bengal) 50

WOMEN'S 'DEVELOPMENT' AND 'PROGRESS' 53

SHARING OF HOUSEWORK AND CHILDCARE 54

AUSTERITY, CHARITY AND ACCUMULATION 56

LAND 58

THE DREAM OF THE MARXISTS 59

MEN ABUSE WOMEN'S BODIES 60

REPRODUCTIVE CONSCIOUSNESS 61

EPILOGUE 62

GLOSSARY 63

BIBLIOGRAPHY 65

ACKNOWLEDGEMENTS

We are born with a debt to our mother, and go through life receiving gifts from innumerable people which benefit and build us in innumerable ways. To the women and men I have had the luck to know and work with, who are labouring to create a new society in the villages of West Bengal, I wish to express my deep gratitude for their friendship and help to me, a European. Their acceptance and affection have been what makes my stay and work here possible.

For providing me shelter as well as introducing me to households and lending me their bicycles, I wish to thank Vikas Kendra staff; for helping me record information and gain a deeper understanding of village life, I owe much to Sabina Yasmin of Atghora. Sandhya Banerjee was a much-needed companion during the later stages of the survey. Rashmoni Mandal and her family looked after me when I was surveying Tribal households at Kutibari and Sri Rampur villages.

To each of the thirty-four households – wife, husband, in-laws and children – I am particularly obliged. You allowed me to observe the private happenings in your home at close quarters, and at the same time, gave your sincere hospitality and cooperation.

Moni Mukherjee of the Centre for Studies in Social Sciences has from the beginning encouraged me, looked over my work and consistently ordered me 'to write.' I am also grateful to Arun Patnaik of the Centre, to Vikraman Nair of the Ananda Bazaar Patrika newspaper and to the staff of Services Centre, especially Julie Chiramal, for their support.

Last but not least, I express my heartfelt thanks to Narinder Bedi of Young India Project for arranging funds (from local sources) which enabled me to undertake this project.

March
1990
Calcutta

To the men: 'On you it depends to be a strong help to the women in the raising of children. Share the women's sorrow.'

The Maiden of the Dakota Legend

About the Author

I am not a Bengali. My birth and education were in Britain, a country that has influenced and been influenced by India. West Bengal was a focal point of British imperialism and strangely I made it my place of 'rebirth' and further education. Over the last decade, I have learnt something of the poverty and problems which burden the people, and how these weigh particularly heavily on village girls and women here. As a woman, I myself have experienced the oppressive hand of patriarchy and felt as blows and insults the culture of a male-dominated and male-adoring society. Poor, illiterate Bengali village youths have assaulted me on the streets, buses and trains, with the same impunity that well-to-do men have similarly treated me, a white middle-class woman. Leftist friends have only the trite words, 'Everything will be alright after the revolution,' to offer as their contribution to the 'gender struggle.' But very early on, it became clear to me that 'the revolution' would in no way be the solution. Socialists in power may put the means of production into the hands of producers, but they would not put the 'means of reproduction' into the hands of reproducers. Theoretically, socialists aim to produce and distribute commodities more efficiently and fairly than capitalists. Mothers create and nurture life itself.

I have seen the tears of village women forbidden outside the house by their husband and that fear of 'What will people say?' And because I am also a woman oppressed by men in some ways, I have felt their suffering keenly. As a qualified homeopath with midwifery training, I have been lucky to come close to that unique experience only women can have of pregnancy and childbirth – the reproductive labour which gives women their female consciousness. Thus, out of my own experiences grew a realization that unless we all become conscious of this unique life-giving and integrative female consciousness, there will never be healthy and lasting social change.

PREFACE

'Once, in a village next to ours, a woman got up at midnight to boil paddy. She was the wife of a wealthy landowner who owned several paan as well as paddy fields. In the morning she would have to feed fifteen labourers who would come to cut the paan leaves. There was no time to lose. She boiled paddy for the rest of the night, sitting next to the hot stove, carrying about heavy buckets of water, lifting out the paddy and spreading it over the yard to dry. She took no rest and had no food. There was no time. She cooked for the fifteen men in the morning, and served them. Before she could rest, have her bath and eat, other tasks needed to be completed, and by the time she had her bath, it was noon. She sat down to eat panta and probably ate too much for her hungry stomach to hold, for she vomited twice and became unconscious. Her wealthy husband had her rushed to hospital where he threw bagfuls of money in front of the doctor, pleading with him to save his wife. They put her on a drip, but it didn't work. She died in the afternoon.'

Recounted by a villager from Diamond Harbour, South 24-Parganas on December 9th 1988.

WHY DISCUSS HOUSEWORK, REPRODUCTION AND CHILDCARE?

It is so obvious that females do housework and care for children and others in the household, that it is simply shocking to realize that **they do not have to** do these tasks. If males shared these tasks with girls and women, then everyone's lives would change drastically. It would bring about a revolution. Let us discuss this truth in the context of West Bengal's rural reality.

Women here spend their whole life doing housework, bearing and caring for children as well as others in their natal and later their husband's households. In many districts (though not in the area I surveyed), women stretch their time and energy to breaking point trying to earn money also.

One could ask, 'So what? Everyone knows this. Why bother to spend time studying, analysing and publicly discussing the issues of housework and childcare? Everyone knows girls and women do all that. They always have. What's so unusual and special about the subject to warrant so much attention?'

Questioning the 'Natural' Laws

Patriarchal attitudes encompass some of the following: that women's natural and primary commitment is to the husband; that women are naturally committed to the maintenance of a home, a family and domestic affairs; that being male means having a commitment to earning for a family and to the outside world; that being female means having to do all the cooking, cleaning, fetching water and looking after everyone; that being male means not having to do all these things; that since this arrangement is Natural and God-given, there is obviously no need to discuss it, let alone change it; that everyone knows it's a man's world, and that women's role is to keep basic needs satisfied, serve men and, naturally, reproduce the species; that freedom, autonomy, power and wealth are meant for men to enjoy and that social and religious laws uphold this Natural and God-given arrangement, as, for example, Manu's law that, from birth till death, a woman should always depend on a man - her father, then her husband and then her son.

In rural West Bengal, the differences between men and women's daily work, social status and expectations for the future are accepted as Natural and God-given because the culture and beliefs of most people are patriarchal. Any challenge to such attitudes is considered threatening and foreign. Feminism generally has a bad name because of its association with threats to the status quo, and it is often disparaged as 'foreign.' However, since other foreign imports do not challenge the patriarchal system, they can be absorbed. For instance, capitalism, Marxism and English medium education do not threaten the status quo and may even strengthen it. But in rural West Bengal, prevailing attitudes dictate that since women have babies, they must be married off, sent away and kept within the house of the husband, and somehow under this system, boys and men are 'naturally' and automatically superior to women too! The way the villagers organise their society reflects what they think about gender differences. Patriarchal attitudes are manifested in every aspect of rural life here and patriarchal practices are justified in the name of being natural and God-given. Thus, change will be very hard to bring about.

The Doctrines of Manu and the religious texts and rites practised in India mostly confirm women's inferiority to men, warn women to obey and serve men and legislate for women's dependence. Challenging something as deep-rooted and ingrained as culture and custom is very difficult, particularly when these are believed by spiritual and faithful people to be laws imposed by an ultimate authority such as Bhagawan, Allah or God. Just as former kings derived their authority to rule from God, rural men in West Bengal derive their authority to rule women. Thus, even discussing that such a set up may be flawed is almost dangerous, and trying to change it could be likened to treason.

Even Marx did not say that women labour in the house, become pregnant, have babies and care for people. (He said 'Men reproduce themselves.') Lenin only made a brief reference to the regrettable 'male right' which forced women to slave in the kitchen. But his was only a brief reference made during the great revolutionary years, and nothing came of it. Since these great men omitted to consider these issues, why should their followers working in West Bengal consider that housework, childcare and reproductive consciousness are important? Frederick Engels, who defined Communist practice as 'from each according to his ability to each according to his need,' also wrote about primary accumulation, which is where women's work must play an important part. Unfortunately, Engels' ideas were rarely adopted by men in their zeal to destroy one form of control for another.

It is regrettable that some of the most progressive elements in society do not discuss women's oppressed condition within patriarchy, let alone devise strategies to change it. To focus attention on the production system only leads ultimately to a strengthening of this system of commodity production and accumulation. It does not revolutionize anything else. To be sure, rural women could be empowered by greater control of economic and productive resources and by a secular and egalitarian legal, educational and health infrastructure. But patriarchal attitudes claiming that males have a God-given superiority to females and that housework and childcare are exclusively women's tasks, will ensure that the fundamental unnaturalness and injustice of contemporary society remain and that the gender-based contradictions between human beings will continue to subtly reproduce themselves like a hidden cancer.

What makes this discussion so acutely necessary also is because struggles for economic justice and women's liberation in rural West Bengal are real and locality specific. Ordinary and often uneducated women as well as some men are challenging the patriarchal as well as the economic structures of their society. My study is a very small part of this collective effort.

BACKGROUND TO THE SURVEY

When I started work on the selection of households to be surveyed, I was completely nonplussed by the number of technical problems facing a single researcher with little statistical training, funds or institutional support.

I wanted to do the following:

1. Gain a better understanding of the male-dominated society as it exists in rural West Bengal, and its effects on women, men and children.
2. Collect accurate data which could be used by others interested in the topic of time and energy spent by different classes and communities of village women in West Bengal.
3. Show that the Marxist theory which relates everything to the method of production and 'class struggle' was a totally inadequate basis from which to launch struggles for social change. Relations between women and men seemed to me to have different origins.
4. Produce a report which could be used by people working in rural areas.

West Bengal has 16 districts and three main communities – Hindu, Muslim and Tribal, although the latter have been Hinduized to a great extent. There are several classes or categories of household living in rural areas, varying with the amount of land cultivated and the profession of the main earning member. Other variables included land and water, that is, the natural environment where the households were situated.

For a comprehensive study I needed several samples, but for accuracy's sake these samples had to be located in the same natural setting, otherwise land tenure and income variables would lose their significance. Thus, I selected the district of North 24-Parganas. Since the water level here is not far below the ground, water is plentiful and the landed peasantry cultivate two or three paddy crops a year as well as many vegetables and oil seeds. Landless labourers find more work here in the North than, for example, South 24-Parganas where the water level is 900 to 1000 feet below ground level. Next, I listed the main categories of household and, with the help of the local people, chose one household from each category and each community for the actual survey.

ORIGINAL MANUSCRIPT

The original manuscript contains nearly 300 pages of information collected from each household on survey day and during interviews held later. A drawing of the structural design of each home is included. The original manuscript contains the following information which has not been included in this report:

1. Dedication;
2. Methodology – survey day, time use accounting and case study writing;
3. Table: 'Activity-wise calorie expenditure per day of rural men, women and children' National Perspective Plan for Women;
4. Census of India 1981 Series 1 'Provisional Population Totals Workers and Non-workers' West Bengal State and 24-Parganas District;
5. Detailed Time Use Accounts of housework activities performed by the different household members on survey day;
6. Detailed Reproductive Histories of each of the wives;
7. Detailed Time Use Accounts of childcare activities performed;
8. Detailed Time Use Accounts of productive (income-earning) activities done within and outside the household;
9. Full quotations of Attitudes to: a) women working outside the households, b) reasons for gender-based division of labour, c) sharing of housework and childcare;
10. Detailed Accounts of activities done by men;
11. Calculations of the Value of each wife's housework and childcare activities;
12. Details of income and expenditure of each household;
13. Details of Cultivation – crops grown, costs of labour and other inputs, attitudes to Minimum Wage and Equal Remuneration Acts, major losses etc.;
14. Time record of when each member of each household was served at each meal;
15. Details of services done in each household – what was done, by and for whom;
16. Details of requests and commands made – what was said, by and to whom;
17. Details of who controls money;
18. Details of who makes the major decisions (in narrative and summarized in tabular form);
19. Details of literacy levels, recreation, food, medical and addiction expenses of wife and husband;
20. Details of Freedom lost or existing for women after puberty and marriage;
21. Perceived problems and solutions of household members;
22. Pro-forma used for the survey (12 pages).

HOUSEHOLDS SURVEYED

Wife's name	Husband's name	H.I. No	Category	Community
Tita	Kartik Mandal	1	Landless labourer	Hindu
Anwara	Himat Ali Mandal	2	Landless labourer	Muslim
Parbati	Dulal Singh	3	Landless labourer	Tribal
Saradini	Tarapada Mandal	4	Marginal farmer	Hindu
Jeebanesa	Abdul Mahid Mandal	5	Marginal farmer	Muslim
Gita	Dinabandhu Singh	6	Marginal farmer	Tribal
Jamuna/Rita	Kr.Krishna Bardhan	7	Small cultivator	Hindu
Halima	Abdur Rab Ahmed	8	Small cultivator	Muslim
Sabitri	Jyotish Singh	9	Small cultivator	Tribal
Krishna	Swapon Biswas	10	Middle cultivator	Hindu
Sherina	Mastali Mandal	11	Middle cultivator	Muslim
Sudha	Nishikanta Ghosh	12	Rich cultivator	Hindu
Firdozi	Jahangir Kabir	13	Rich cultivator	Muslim
Dipali	Dhiren Ghosh	14	Big landowner	Hindu
Manwara/Taslim	Asraf Ali Hussain	15	Big landowner	Muslim
Sandhya	Haran Mandal	16	Brickfield worker	Hindu
Esmatara	Rahim Mandal	17	Brickfield worker	Muslim
Purnima	Tapos Mandal	18	Van-rickshaw puller	Hindu
Jayda	Sukur Ali Mandal	19	Van-rickshaw puller	Muslim
Namita	Biram Singh	20	Van-rickshaw puller	Tribal
Anima	Bimal Ghosh	21	Service-holder	Hindu
Rokeya	Sefa Uddin Mandal	22	Service-holder	Muslim
Puspa	Sudhir Ray	23	Service-holder	Tribal
Suchitra	Naba Kr. Mandal	24	Teacher	Hindu
Sufia	Abdur Samed Ahmed	25	Teacher	Muslim
Renuka	Prabhat Pal	26	Business	Hindu
Latifa	Salaam	27	Deed-writer	Muslim
Reba	Tapos Ray	28	Money-lender	Hindu
Rizia	Surat Ali Sardar	29	Money-lender	Muslim
Chintarani	Kanak Pal	30	Artisan	Hindu
Aleya	Jamat Ali Mandal	31	Artisan	Muslim
Sumitra	Manmata Haldar	32	Fisherman	Hindu
Kahinoor/Sakina	Saheed Ali Mandal	33	Animal husbandry	Muslim
Sandhya	Ranjit Sardar	34	Animal husbandry	Hindu/Tribal

H.I. No.: Household Identification Number

FINDINGS OF THE SURVEY

Mine was a micro-level study with only a single sample from each category and community; altogether 34 case studies. Only a macro-level study of similar intensity could provide enough data for drawing more statistically accurate conclusions about conditions in rural West Bengal. However, within the limits of the framework, some significant points can be made. I have divided the main conclusions into two sections:

A. HOUSEWORK
B. REPRODUCTION AND CHILDCARE

A. HOUSEWORK

1. Women spend more time and energy on housework than men

The survey bore out a well-known fact that the involvement in terms of hours and energy spent on life-maintaining activities is much greater in the case of girls and women than boys and men. Data from the 34 households has been summarised in the following tables:

Table 1 - Range of Time spent on Housework by Wives and Husbands;
Table 2 - Range of Time spent on Housework by other Females and Males;
Table 3 - Range of Time spent on Housework by Domestic Workers;
Table 4 - Average Time spent on Housework by Wives, Husbands, other Females and Males and Domestic Workers

Table 1   Range of Time spent on Housework by Wives and Husbands

Range of time spent	Number of Wives	Number of Husbands
No time at all	0	20
Up to 1 hour	0	8
1 to 2 hours	0	2
2 to 4 hours	9	0
4 to 6 hours	11	0
6 to 8 hours	10	0
8 to 10 hours	4	0
	34	32

NB. Manwara and Taslima's (15) and Sakina and Kahinoor's (33) Housework Time has been calculated as an average of both women's time spent. Mat-making of Older and Younger Kakis and Rabia (15) has been excluded. Naba Kumar (24) mended electricity line at home for approximately 3 hours. This time has been excluded. Kumar Krishna (7) and Jamat Ali (31) were absent on Survey Day.

Table 2   Range of Time spent on Housework by other Females and Males (members of the family)

Range of time spent	Number of Females	Number of Males
Up to 1 hour	3	10
1 to 2 hours	5	1
2 to 4 hours	7	1
4 to 6 hours	3	0
6 to 8 hours	1	0
8 to 10 hours	2	0
10 to 12 hours	10	0
12 to 14 hours	1	0
	32	12

NB. 'Children' of one household worked for 30 mins. This time has been excluded. Mother-in-law was present in 8 households. Each one did some housework. Asraf's father (15) has two wives.

Table 3   Range of Time spent on Housework by Domestic Workers (all Female except one)

Range of time spent	Number
Up to 1 hour	2
1 to 2 hours	1
2 to 4 hours	3
4 to 6 hours	1
	7

Table 4 Average Time spent on Housework by Wives, Husbands, other females and Males and Domestic Workers

Average Time	Persons	Percentage of Average Time
6 hours 11 mins.	Wives	45.5
18 mins.	Husbands	2.3
4 hours 1 min.	Other Females	29.5
33 mins.	Other Males	4.0
2 hours 32 mins.	Domestics	18.7

2. Males are averse to doing housework

Some of the typical responses of men to the question, 'Would you be willing to share housework equally with women when you are at home?' or which were expressed in the course of conversation, included:

'These are women's tasks.'
'People would laugh if they saw me doing the cooking.'
'Boys don't do the washing up.'

'Would women plough the fields?'
'Would women do men's work?'
'Men have no time.'
'Women have come into this world to serve their husband. Therefore, serving the husband is women's religion.'

Many women's responses reflected this attitude also. Patriarchal values are not perpetrated by force only. Many women also believe their 'rightful' place is in the home.

Women's labour in the household gives men free time. Men are obviously aware of the benefits of this sex-based division of labour. What has become a privilege acquired by force perpetuates itself as a 'natural' or 'God-given' matter. 'Housework is women's work' is a concept only, but it is made real by the powerlessness of women divided up by patriarchal marriage arrangements and by social and cultural customs.

3. There are exceptional men who do housework and childcare

Sefa (22), Kanak (30) and Ranjit (34) prove that men in rural West Bengal can share housework and childcare. Paucity of examples prevents me from drawing any conclusion, yet I feel that class and community are not factors which determine whether men share housework and childcare with women or not. Sefa is a Muslim service-holder, Kanak a poor Hindu artisan and Ranjit a Tribal fisherman.

4. Women want men to share housework and childcare equally

In response to the question, 'Would it be convenient if men share housework and childcare equally with women?' 26 wives said it would and 7 said it would not be. Reasons given by those who approved of and others who disapproved of sharing are given below.

Wives who approved	Reason given
Tita	The upper/lower, owner/labourer relations would not exist.
Parbati	When I can't manage then I ask him, but I love it when he does it without my asking.
Sardini	It would help us to finish the work quickly so we could all go to the fields.
Jeebanesa	We could both share the burdens equally.
Jamuna	He'd understand what I've been doing and not complain.
Halima	We'd get the chance to go outside.
Sabitri	...but men would not agree to.
Krishna	Neither would have more or less work than the other.
Firdozi	If they do, women will become somewhat liberated from their prisoner's existence.
Dipali	We could get some rest. There's no time to go out. If they help it would be really useful.
Esmatara	We have so much to do that if he helped me, it would save time.
Purnima	But then they'd tell us to go and cut paddy!

Jayda	If women work outside with men and men work with women in the house then the mutual understanding is good.
Namita	Actually, we have to do it alone.
Anima	Our difficulties would be less.
Puspa	Everyone ought to do housework and childcare.
Suchitra	Relations between husband and wife would improve.
Sufia	We'll be able to earn if he helps us.
Latifa	It (the work) would be done faster and husband and wife could rest sooner.
Reba	Difficulties would be reduced. I would be able to make mats, sweaters and covers in the extra time (for household use.)
Rizia	...because we'd be able to go out (spoken with a sigh.)
Chintarani	If we don't work together, we can't understand each other's needs.
Sumitra	If he shared I'd be able to do some other work.
Sakina	Women would become a bit freer.
Sandhya	If I go anywhere, when I come back, I'd find everything's been done.

Wives who disapproved	Reasons given
Anwara	It would be a sin to tell him to do housework.
Gita	Men would suffer if they had to do housework.
Manwara	It's just impossible.
Sandhaya Mendal	Men don't find time.
Renuka	Girls will have to do it...Perhaps it would be a bit convenient.

Suda and Taslima both disapproved also.

5. Males and mothers-in-law believe that only females ought to do housework and childcare

Apart from husbands, other young and older men felt that only girls and women ought to do these tasks. The following table has been compiled from the responses made to the question, 'Who do you think ought to do housework and childcare?'

Table 5

Possible answer	Wife	Husband	Mother-in-law	Father-in-law	Mature girl	Mature boy
Only girls and women ought to do housework & childcare	8	24	6	4	1	8
Females and males ought to share these tasks equally	28	9	1	1	8	5

One reason mothers-in-law believed the wife should do the work was because she herself had worked hard until her son's marriage, and now felt it was the turn of the younger woman. Another reason was pity for the son who had to work outside. Though several young men expressed the view that housework and childcare should be shared equally, this was rarely put into practice. Neither community background, nor class or occupation was a significant factor in determining any of the attitudes. The only determining factor seemed to be the gender of the respondent.

6. Women who have never worked outside have various opinions about the causes of the sex-based division of labour.

The question, 'Why do women work inside the household and men outside?' was generally answered after a puzzled hesitation. The gender-based division of labour appears as natural as the need to eat and sleep! After thinking carefully, 20 wives said it was due to social norms which had become established over the years. Other replies included:

- 'Women are women and men are men.'
- 'It is bad for women to go outside.'
- 'It is Allah's will.'

7. Women want to earn

In response to the question, 'What is your attitude to women working outside the household?' 30 women expressed their approval, but then 10 qualified this by saying they would not work 'in the fields or market.' Four women had already gained experience working outside. Six strongly disapproved of the idea.

The double burden of an earning woman who also has to do all the housework and childcare can only be overcome if the husband and other males in the household throw off their prejudices and share these tasks with the women. Also, men can only overcome physiological and psychological 'distance' from the reproductive and nurturing processes if they consciously integrate themselves into these processes by actively and joyfully sharing all the domestic labour.

Women who would never work outside:

Saradini and Sumitra (only in the family's field), Dipali, Esmatara, Purnima, Anima, Suchitra, Sufia, Rizia

Women who would work outside 'but only behind purdah':

Halima, Taslima, Aleya, Kahinoor

Women who would never work outside:

Anwara: 'Not even if I had to starve.'
Sherina: 'Never, unless I'm forced to by my husband's death.'
Manwara, Sandhya Mandal, Latifa, Reba

Women who had worked outside already:

Parbati, Jayda, Namita, Sandhya Sardar

8. A creche in the village would be useful

A creche is an important social asset for when neither parent nor anybody else is at home. 66 wives and husbands said that a crèche (balwadi) would be useful. Only Renuka (26) and Tapos (18) said it would not. The establishment of crèches in villages and at work sites should not merely remain as a policy decision on paper but needs to be implemented. Working women often carry their children while they work.

9. The workload of both wife and husband increased after marriage

This was true for everyone except 2 husbands. More women than men said they would never have married if they had been given the choice. The workload of the wife increased markedly after the delivery of her first baby. The workload of the mother-in-law decreased markedly after the arrival of her son's wife. It might be said that the gender-based division of labour itself perpetuates patriarchy by ensuring that the husband's mother has a strong self-interest in bringing a daughter-in-law into her household. After a lifetime of what could be considered slave labour, the older woman looks forward to 'retirement', and expects as a right, that the young woman will take over the housework.

Firdozi's mother-in-law (13) said, 'I was doing this work until my son married so I want his wife to spend her life doing housework now.'

Before marriage, men's domestic needs are met by their mother and sisters. At most, men wash their own clothes and make their own bed. After marriage, the wife is expected to do these tasks, while the men's work outside increases.

10. Little girls have less time to play and study than their brothers

The sex-based division of labour means that, even at their parents' house long before marriage, little girls' time and energy are spent on domestic labour, while their brothers are free to play and to study.

Sabha (24) was sweeping while her three brothers studied. At school, she is in a lower class than she should be for her age. Parbati (3) has harmed her daughter irrevocably by making Kalyani (but never her son Krishna) take out the goats, fetch water and cook. Sagari (16) is still struggling to make her future, torn between her mother's orders to look after the goats, and her own desire to study.

11. Larger households and land-holdings mean more work for women

While the outside work of male property owners tends to be supervisory, the work of women inside becomes increasingly physically laborious with the increasing size of the property. Time and energy spent on cleaning increases with the house and yard size, amount of utensils and clothes. Cooking takes longer when there is money to buy and prepare varieties of foods, and when there are many labourers to cook for. Time and energy spent on food processing increases when there is more land. Employed domestic workers reduced the burden of housework and childcare for some women like Firdozi (13) and Dipali (14), but their husbands were completely relieved of all physical labour by the agricultural labourers they employed. In keeping with the social attitude to domestic work, the rate of pay for a month's housework and childcare by Lakhi (10), a young female domestic, was Rs4/- with two free meals a day. However, in the same area, an agricultural labourer earns from Rs.300/- to Rs.700/- per month with two free meals a day.

12. Few protests

Girls' upbringing and women's lack of independence mean they provide a docile supply of labour which is both unpaid and of unlimited hours. Even the most odious tasks are done without a murmur. The wife of a high school headmaster throws away her husband's night urine the following morning; when the concrete latrine was cleaned in two households, it was the wife who did this in both cases, even though one of them is used only by the husband.

Protests are rare, and when made, rather harmless. Powerless and without the weapon of unionized labour (the strike), a common form of protest is one which hurts the girl or woman herself, as for example, when Sagari refused to eat at night because her mother had told her to take out and fetch the goats when she wanted to study (16.)Fasting was a way of expressing her grief and anger and, perhaps, of doing something independently and controlling something in her life herself. Sagari's mother had complained about her daughter's worthlessness, an attitude that clashed with the growing girl's own sense of worth, especially since she had come first in class.

In Kalyani's case, at first, she refused to obey both her mother and brother when they told her to see to the goats (3). 'Only if you pay me,' she said. 'Don't ask me to work unless you pay me.' Suchitra (24) refused to wash her husband's clothes after an argument. Sakina (33) who never ever went to the market, had asked her husband to bring back a sari for her from the market after selling some chickens. When he didn't bring her the sari, she could only burst out crying helplessly and threaten not to look after the chickens any longer. Apart from that and some grumbling, however, she could do nothing. When it was suggested that she take the chickens to sell at the market, she said that society would not allow this and that she would be too shy anyway. However, when Dipali (14) cannot tolerate being inside the house any longer, she defies her husband's orders not to go out. Perhaps such disobedience is possible because she is no longer young and has a daughter-in-law who looks after things when she is out.

13. Women use up much energy at work

In the study, a rough indication of the amount of energy women used as they worked throughout the day was made by recording the number and type of water vessels carried and the distance walked to the tube well or pond. One large kolshi weighs about 7 kilos when full of water. Bundles of firewood were not weighed. One large sack of paddy weighs approximately 50 kilos.

The reason for attempting an approximate measurement of energy consumed was to establish that, just as men labour hard on the fields, the work done by women for the household is also very laborious and energy consuming. Women have an added burden when they become pregnant and during the breast-feeding period. The majority of women surveyed got no rest during the last month of pregnancy and very few got any extra food. Some women's food was even restricted during pregnancy and after delivery.

Village men are served first even when the wife is pregnant. It is generally believed that men need more food than women because they are said to work harder than women. However, a pregnant woman needs as much food as a man and even more protein, carbohydrates and fatty foods when breast-feeding. That they do not get this is possibly a reason for big differences in height and weight between men and women here.

Cooking and washing clothes are activities which all village women do. Processing paddy was done by two-thirds of the women in my survey. Although village women are considered non-workers by the Government of India Census, their work is in fact very intensive, laborious and time-consuming, as the following descriptions show.

Cooking

1. Fuel is fetched by the cook either from outside or from a store, and put at the side of the stove. When needed, the cook gets up to collect more, which she may do several times before the cooking is finished. She keeps the stove alight by replenishing it regularly with fuel. This may also be done by another woman or young girl.

2. The cook needs to fetch a flame, either a lamp or match and box, or sometimes a lighted piece of fuel like a stick from a neighbour's stove. She fetches matches from her husband or father-in-law (if they are smokers.) If the stove goes out, she has to repeat the same process.

3. Water for cooking and washing utensils and vegetables needs to be fetched and placed in a convenient position. Women become adept at managing with a minimum of water and yet preserving high standards of cleanliness. Some women prefer to use pond water for cooking. Jeebanesa walked 500 feet to a particular pond to fetch water for boiling rice.

4. Cooking rice involves the following stages:
- fetching it from the store;
- washing it either at the tube well or with water in the kitchen;
- putting the rice on to boil and seeing that it does not boil over;
- taking the heavy pot off the stove, tipping it upside down after carefully adjusting the lid to let the starchy water drain away;
- shaking the pot to settle the rice and putting it on a shelf.

5. Preparing one curry involves the following stages:
- fetching the vegetables either from the store or field. Sherina's niece climbed a tree to harvest edible shoots.
- getting out the cutter. The cook may need to fetch one from a neighbour if she does not have her own. The boti is fixed into a narrow wooden base and curves up so the cook squats holding the vegetable in both hands to cut or peel it. This knife is used for cutting meat and scaling fish as well.

6. Spice preparation takes up more time and energy. Powdered spices are generally not purchased. The cook saves money by crushing the original ingredient herself. Taking out a heavy stone grinder, the cook carefully places each spice on an even heavier flat stone and rolls the grinder over it adding a little water. She skilfully gathers up the spicy juices into separate piles, perhaps putting them on to different saucers, rinses the utensils and puts them away. When crushing red chillies, fingers are made sore by the 'jhal.' Wealthier households eat several curries made from varieties of fish, meat and vegetables and each is prepared with different spice combinations. Dal and chutney may also be made.

Cooks get used to cut fingers and burns from handling hot fuel, pots and chillies. Sharp bones get stuck behind nails when fish is cut or washed. Scalding from hot oil and boiling water while making tea or rice, or from upturned curry as it is stirred in a squatting position, as well as severe burns when long sari ends catch fire – are not uncommon occupational health hazards for cooks in the village of North 24-Parganas. From their early years, young girls and women are exposed to dangerously high concentrations of carbon monoxide and other poisonous gases while cooking. The World Health Organisation states that maximum exposure of pollutants should not exceed 150 micrograms per cubic metre. Village women are exposed to 45 times this amount. Pollution is worsened by monsoon and winter weather when the damp cold air becomes heavy.

Laundry

On the day when the bulk of the clothes are washed, the following stages are involved:
1. Dirty clothes are collected from around the house and put in the yard;
2. The woman fetches water and pours it into a korai which she places over the yard stove. She may need to fetch a korai from the neighbours and return it later;
3. She collects fuel and puts it into and beside the stove;
4. She lights the fuel and puts the clothes into the water as it heats;
5. She fetches washing powder from the house or shop and adds this;
6. With a long stick, she moves the clothes around in the boiling water;
7. After some time, she fetches a large basket, hauls out the hot wet clothes with the stick and puts them into the basket;
8. She then carries the loaded basket to the pond;
9. At the pond, she takes out one piece of clothing and bangs it on a piece of flat stone, using one or both of her arms and the upper part of her body in a regular forward and backward motion. This is repeated for each piece of clothing – sari, dhoti, shirt, petticoat, lungi, towel, shawl, sheet...
10. The clothing is rinsed in the pond and put back in the basket;
11. She carries the basket back and putting it down in the yard, hangs out everything over the bamboo line, the roof or nearby bushes. She lays out clothes to dry on grass if the space for hanging clothes is insufficient.

In summer if ponds near the house dry up, women have to take the laundry further to find better ponds or do the scrubbing and banging of the clothes at the tube well and pump all the water necessary for rinsing. During the monsoon, she has to take clothes off the line when it starts to rain, arrange them inside and then take them out again when the sun shines. Clothes get dirty more quickly during winter.

12. Once the clothes are dry, she takes them off the line, folds them and puts them away inside on bamboo poles or shelves.

Anima washed Bimal's shawl and left it out to dry. On his return home, he snatched it from the line without comment or any sign of appreciation. A common command of the husband to their wives was to be given a clean towel or clothes. These products are in demand but the labour involved rarely acknowledged.

Processing paddy

Approximately two days are needed to process one sack of paddy. The heavy work of boiling paddy is done in the morning, the drying is done during the day and the paddy is put into sacks and stored in the evening.

1. The woman rises earlier than usual and brings out one or two sacks of paddy;
2. She pours some paddy into a couple of large earthenware bowls over a stove in the yard, which she lights;
3. Throughout the morning, she fetches several buckets of water which she pours over the steaming paddy;
4. She keeps the stove alight by fuelling it regularly, replenishing fuel as it gets used up;
5. Once the paddy has been heated for long enough, she scoops it out and spreads it over the yard using her feet or, perhaps, a rake;
6. The drying process starts and as the sun mounts, she moves the grains with her feet to ensure they are exposed;
7. Constant watch has to be kept to ensure that chickens and other birds do not peck at the paddy - which is all very precious to the household, especially if it has been purchased and the family is poor. Children may help to shoo away animals and birds.
8. When the paddy has dried, the woman piles it up neatly by sweeping in circles, carefully separating the grains from the dust;
9. She then transfers the paddy into a sack which she has mended beforehand, if necessary;
10. Cleaning the paddy is another laborious job which may be left for the following day. After pouring out a measure of the paddy which she boiled and dried earlier, the woman squats with a winnowing tray and starts to sift. With dextrous jerks, she separates the grains from the chaff, repeating this pouring and sifting until the whole sack has been cleaned;
11. Then she puts the cleaned paddy back into the sack, keeping the chaff separately. This is usedas fuel.
12. With help, she sews up the sack and carries it to the storage place;

Women usually wear a cloth over their head to keep the dust out of their hair. One sack of processed paddy sells for around Rs.150/- which money is generally handled only by the husband who sells the paddy at the market.

---

14. The value of women's housework and childcare is enormous

In the Government of India's 1981 Census, rural Bengali women were categorised as 'non-workers' even though non-government surveys claim that rural women's unpaid work inside and outside the home contributes nearly 50% to the Net Domestic Product of India. The Deputy Registrar Generalof Census, Rama Rao, confirmed that in the 1991 Census housework and childcare would againremain unrecorded. Mr. Rao said that if the government were to record housework and childcare, 'it would mean women are rich.' This interesting statement reveals the conundrum caused by a money-based system where productivity and wealth are only valuable if they can be measured in terms of money. Thus, 'women's work' being unpaid is rendered valueless, even while it is essential to the survival of human society and requires women's lifelong time and energy.

Simultaneously, the gender-based division of labour (with a culture that demands the sacrifice, dependence and inferior status of women) where men are paid for their work but women aren't paid for theirs, inevitably leads to the enslavement of females IN ORDER THAT males can be wealthy and omnipotent. Mr. Rao's statement also reveals an understanding of the worth of women's unpaid labour: if, and it is an infinitely big IF, women were paid for the work they do, then they would be rich. However, it is unlikely that the slave-owners will face an uprising or be forced to give up their ill-gotten gains any time soon, so their accountants can refuse to record the inherent value of the slaves' work and, with a laugh, the ignorant, arrogant and greedy can dismiss housework and childcare as worthless with the same scorn that patriarchs dismiss the potential challenge of female autonomy.

However, Mr. Rao was pleased to point out to me the addition, in the 1991 Individual Slip pro-forma for collecting details of each household member's work, of the words in brackets: '...including unpaid work on farm or in family enterprise' under the old question, 'Did you work any time at all last year?' This small addition, in brackets, is the result of years of pressure from women activists and academics who have pressed for official recognition of women's unpaid work which 'increases the household's command over the necessities.' Such work could include preparing paddy for sale and working on the family field if produce were to be sold. Yet housework and childcare would still remain outside the purview of the Indian Census as it does from most national accounting systems.

I am not unaware of the difficulties of evaluating work whose 'products', like meals, clean clothes or children, are not sold, although seven sophisticated methods have been developed to try to evaluate housework and childcare in urban societies. However, while each method has its uses, each is also fraught with problems too. Really what is required is an awareness of the day-to-day reality of women's lives and greater government investment in a low-cost rural electricity and gas energy network and in rural people's health and education.

<u>A rough evaluation of women's work</u>

I used two methods in my attempt to give monetary value to the housework and childcare done by the wives surveyed:

1. The payment in cash and kind which is made to employed domestic workers in the area, or which the husband (as the earning person) would be willing to pay someone for doing the work his wife does without pay.

2. The potential monetary value of work the wife could do outside i.e. if she did not have to spend her time and energy doing housework and childcare, how much she could earn, either from daily labour, business, tuitions or whatever she is qualified for and willing to do.

The purpose of this particular account is twofold:

1. To highlight that women's housework and childcare have got value, and that this must be recognised by women themselves, their families, village society and the government.

2. To increase the confidence of women once their work is publicly recognised, and to increase the participation of men in housework and childcare when the value of these activities is recognised and their prestige grows.

It was seen during the survey that the domestic work of women is essential to the existence of all categories and communities of household. Not only does her labour fulfil everybody's basic needs, but because it is unpaid, each household saves money. When a man says he would pay an outsider Rs.300/- per month for doing the work his wife does for free, he is acknowledging his minimum debt to his wife. It is his debt to her because he can accumulate (money, land, possessions, political power and prestige) at the cost of her freedom.

However, what is not accounted for is another unpaid contribution which the wife makes as mother of his children. An employee domestic would not become pregnant, give birth and raise her employer's children. The child bears the name of the father and grows up in the father's house. Socially, the child is acknowledged as the father's, a possession of the father and, culturally, the mother's role is rendered almost invisible, her body and mind owned and exploited by the man (and his family.)

Evaluating housework and childcare is so difficult precisely because these are tasks which do not bring in money. Men created the money system and so they have ensured that they do the tasks which earn them money, while women do the tasks which are unpaid or badly paid. Men do a great deal of cooking and washing up and serving, but in restaurants, where they are paid. These same tasks men refuse to do in the house. Similarly, men forbid women to cook and wash and serve in restaurants where they could earn money.

Various factors made it very difficult to calculate the 'potential monetary value of work women could do outside.' For instance, some women were unwilling to work outside the household at all, making any assessment of 'the value of work they could do outside' impossible. Also, many women who would not work as agricultural labourers, domestic workers or vendors, would work 'behind purdah' or at a 'respectable' job, but could not do so because they lacked the necessary education and skills. Thirdly, for several months, there is no regular work even for men who depend on agricultural labour, and, finally, many men would never allow 'their' women to work outside.

An estimate of the possible potential monetary value of each of the wives' work is given in the Original Manuscript and collated data is given below:

Table 6   Range of payment husband would give to a domestic worker for doing the work his wife does unpaid i.e. savings for the household

a) Excluding the value of food and clothes i.e. these would be provided free of cost.

Rs. per month	Number of husbands
0 – 50	3
51 – 100	3
101 – 200	2
201 – 300	3
301 – 400	2
Above 400	1
	14

b) Including the value of food and clothes provided by the employer

Rs. per month	Number of husbands
0 – 50	2
51 – 100	0
101 – 200	3
201 – 300	7
301 – 400	2
401 – 500	3
501 – 600	0
601 – 700	1
Above 700	2
	20

Table 7   Average payment husband would give a domestic worker i.e. average saving for households made by wives' free labour

a) Exclusive of food and clothes   Rs.225/- per month
b) Inclusive of food and clothes   Rs.421/- per month

Note:
Total housework and childcare also includes the labour of other females in the household who, therefore, also contribute to savings.

Table 8   Range of monthly income of husbands

Amount earned (Rs.)	Number of men	% of total
Up to 300	5	14.7
301 – 500	5	14.7
501 – 700	3	8.8
701 – 1,000	5	14.7
1,001 – 1,500	6	17.7
1,501 – 2,000	3	8.8
2,001 – 2,500	4	11.8
Over 2,500	3	8.8
	34	100.0

The Hindu custom of giving dowry, though unlawful, has spread to the Muslim community also, and in recent years, the value of gifts has increased.

Table 9   Cash and articles given at marriage

H.I. No.	To husbands by wife's family	To wives by husband's family
1	Utensils	/
2	Bicycle, wedding garments, Rs.50/- broker's fee, Rs.200/-	/
3	/	/
4	/	/
5	'Gifts', utensils	/
6	Utensils	/
7	/	/
8	Gold earrings, bicycle, poultry, goats, utensils, grinding board, stone pestle and mortar	/
9	/	Rs.7/-
10	Watch, bicycle, metal utensils,	

	jewellery set	/
11	Watch, bicycle, golden buttons and bracelets	/
12	/	Rs.600/-
13	/	Jewellery
14	/	/
15	'Some articles', jewellery, Rs.1,500/-	/
16	/	Earrings, bangles
17	/	/
18	Rs. 3,000/-	/
19	/	/
20	/	/
21	Rs. 10,000/-, copper, brass and gold utensils, bicycle, watch. Total value Rs.15,000/-.	/
22	Rs. 2,000/-, bicycle, watch, jewellery, gold	/
23	/	Rs.40/-
24	Jewellery	/
25	Jewellery set, bicycle, watch	/
26	/	/
27	Bicycle, watch, jewellery	/
28	/	/
29	/	Rs. 42/-
30	Metal utensil, gold, jewellery	/
31	/	/
32	/	/
33	/	/
34	/	/

Note:
Bride price used to be given at Muslim and Tribal marriages;
Wife's jewellery is mortgaged when husband takes a loan;
Some women continue to bring vegetables and poultry from their parents' household, for example, Anwara (2) and Esmatara (17)

<u>Analysis of community and gifts at marriage</u>

Number of Hindu married couples   = 14
Number of Muslim married couples   = 14
Number of Tribal married couples   = 5
Number of Hindu + Tribal married couples   = 1

Number of women who gave to men		%age of women who gave to men
Hindu	6	43%
Muslim	8	57%
Tribal	1	20%

Number of men who gave to women		%age of men who gave to women
Hindu	2	14%
Muslim	2	14%
Tribal	2	40%

Number of couples who gave no gifts		Percentage
Hindu	6	43%
Muslim	4	29%
Tribal	2	40%

Hindu + Tribal couple exchanged no gifts

15. Wives' free housework and childcare as well as the dowry they bring help accumulation to take place in the husband's household

The example of Anima and Bimal (21) illustrates this well. Given that her dowry was more than twice Bimal's annual salary as a postman, Anima was a big boost to his household's economy assoon as she entered it. Apart from this, according to Bimal's own calculations, Anima saves him Rs.8,400/- per year by doing housework and childcare for free. (This does not include the expenseof feeding and clothing her.) Thus, Bimal is able to save whatever he earns and Anima more than redoubles her dowry's value every two years by working constantly inside the household and caring for the child. Half of the households surveyed could be analysed similarly.

16. Male supremacy is the main factor determining family power structure

The land and house are in the husband's or his family's name. He eats first, services are done for him, he gives orders and makes the major decisions. If there is only one small bed, he will sleep onit. The survey revealed that male supremacy is the basis of the economic, social and cultural life of each household, except Sandhya and Ranjit's (34) where Sandhya is Hindu and Ranjit is Tribal.

The salient points have been summarised below.

<u>Land tenure</u>

The land tenure was in the husband's name. The only exceptions were:
i) H.I. 15 where it was in Asraf's, his father's, mother's and some in his wives' names. The mango grove was cultivated by sharecroppers who took 50% of the fruit. Half the grove was in his name and half in his father's.
ii) Bimal registered a fraction of his brother's land in Anima's name.

<u>Eating order</u>

The wife served her husband or in-laws first and herself last. The only exceptions were:
i) Krishna (10) ate before her husband at night when he was out, but she had served out and covered his food, making it ready for him to take on his return.
ii) Young Muslim boys being trained as maulovi at the local mosque were always served first (11.)
iii) Firdozi (13) ate her noon meal 10 minutes before her husband.
iv) Kanak (30) served the night meal but ate before his wife.
v) Ranjit (34) served himself on his return from work.

The table below has been compiled from a detailed record of serving times of each household member at each meal observed on the survey day.

Table 10

H.I. No.	Meal	Number of minutes husband was served before wife
1	Night	42 minutes
2	Night	35 minutes
3	Night	17 minutes
4	Night	25 minutes
5		Wife was fasting for Ramadan
6	Night	15 minutes
7		Wife was absent
8	Night	6 minutes
9	Noon	2 hours 37 minutes. Husband was out in evening.
10	Noon	25 minutes. Husband was out in evening.
11	Night	26 minutes
12	Night	1 hour 35 minutes
13	Noon	Wife ate 10 minutes before husband. Night meal unseen.
14	Night	5 minutes
15		All were fasting for Ramadan
16	Night	23 minutes
17	Night	18 minutes
18	Night	13 minutes
19	Noon	1 hour 15 minutes. Husband was out at night.
20	Noon	14 minutes. Husband was out at night.
21	Night	2 minutes
22	Night	1 hour 56 minutes
23	Noon	Wife started before husband who was drinking tari. She did not eat at night.
24	Noon	10 minutes. At night, husband told her to eat first.
25	Late morning	26 minutes. Night meal unseen
26	Night	16 minutes
27	Night	10 minutes. Daughter-in-law who was serving ate 45 minutes after her father-in-law.
28	Night	24 minutes
29	Night	21 minutes
30	Night	18 minutes
31		Husband was absent
32	Night	11 minutes
33	Night	26 minutes (1st wife), 21 minutes (2nd wife)
34		Wife ate first at each meal

Services   Table 11

Services done for household members	Number of times
Wife for husband	38
Husband for wife	3
Female for male	34
Male for female	8
Female for female	16
Male for male	3

Note: Services for neighbours and by children for parents have been excluded. Commands

Table 12

Commands given by household members	Number of times
Wife to husband	52
Husband to wife	101
Female to male	128
Male to female	141
Female to female	400
Male to male	47

Control over money

Money earned by Hindu and Muslim women from within the household could be spent by them only if a vendor came to the house. Otherwise, they gave it to the husband and told him what was needed from the market. None of the Hindu or Muslim women went to the local shop or large village market, except Sumitra (32), a Scheduled Caste woman who went to the local shop, and Sandhya (34) (a Caste Hindu married to a Tribal man) who actually did the shopping. She became annoyed when Ranjit took money without asking her, especially since she knew it would be spent on tari. However, all the other Hindu and Muslim women accepted that they had no control over money outside the precincts of the household. The older Tribal women like Gita (6) and Puspa (23) went to the large village market alone and the younger Namita (20) could buy provisions from the local shop.

Bank and Post Office accounts were all in the husband's name.

Illustrative of an unpublicised form of exploitation is an incident witnessed at Kahinoor's and Sakina's household (33.) On survey day, Sakina spent 28 minutes looking after the chickens and 48 minutes for the goats. Presumably, she would spend similar time and energy everyday. The animals were taken to the market to be sold by Saheed, the husband. On this day, he took several chickens to the market and would have made nearly Rs.200/- because he sold them all. Sakina had requested him to buy her a sari and blouse since she wanted to visit her daughter-in-law's house the following day. Saheed returned in the evening with some sweets and provisions for the night meal, but he had not purchased Sakina's sari or blouse. Badly shocked and disappointed, Sakina burst into tears and cried out, 'I shall stop keeping chickens if I don't get anything. I don't get a paisa for my work...!' She kept repeating desperately that she had asked him to get her a sari. 'It was <u>my</u> money! Looking after chickens all day in the mud...' she blurted out, weeping uncontrollably. Her daughter-in-law and Kahinoor told her to be quiet, but when I suggested that Sakina should be allowed to express herself, Kahinoor told me, 'We've been cheated all our lives. Got nothing for the goats and chickens he's sold.'

I would contradict the Marxists, of whom there are many in West Bengal, who believe that patriarchy will disappear with the end of feudal and capitalist material structures and the arrival of the socialist revolution. Certain religious teachings and cultural practices have evolved attitudes which promote unjust treatment of women. Such attitudes can be held in any material structure since they are rooted in faith and obedience to authority which exists outside or beyond the material realm.

In the above case, a man is able to hurt, ignore and exploit women just because he is a man and they are women. And the question which needs to be asked if we are to move on from such a situation is, 'Why have men needed to create such a set-up where they can hurt, ignore and exploit women with total impunity?' Simple greed and bloody-mindedness could be one answer. Another could be because they have a very deep insecurity about their own worth, and, to the Marxists and many others, I would say that the roots of this lack of self-worth are buried, not in the sphere of production and the material structures, but in the psychology of men – in their deep fear of alienation, insignificance and lack of worth caused by their role in the sphere of species reproduction.

Decision-making

Table 13   Household members who make the main decision

Decision	Joint	Wife	Husband	Others	Not made
Whether to take dowry	16	3	9	5	1
Whether to give dowry	16	3	8	6	1
About children's studies	16	5	9	3	1
About buying/selling property	14	1	12	6	1
Accepting a love or inter-communal marriage in the family	19	1	5	7	2
Whether wife can visit parents	6	5	7	5	11

17. Male comfort, enjoyment and privilege are the main factors determining the allocation of resources in the household

The survey showed that men are more qualified and they are freer to participate in social and cultural functions than women. Since they control money, men can and do invest it largely in themselves and property. These features exist irrespective of class or community background. Even the poorest men are better-off than their wives. The tables below summarize the main findings, details of which are given in the original manuscript.

Table 14   Outside recreation of wives and husbands

a) In most cases, the number of times jatra, cinema and fairs attended is more in the case of husbands than wives.
b) Men are free to visit friends' homes, but usually married women are not.
c) Muslim men attend fewer recreational functions than Hindu or Tribal men.
d) Muslim women attend least of all.
e) Men attend general village and political party meetings, while women only attend women's meetings organised by local voluntary societies.
f) Attendance at meetings: Wives   -   4
                              Husbands -   23

Table 15   Average expense incurred on clothing the previous year

Wives' clothing   Rs. 374/-   NB: Jamat Ali's (31) clothing expense was
Husbands' clothing   Rs. 502/-   not found out due to his frequent absence

Table 16   Literacy levels of wives and husbands

Level	No. of wives	No. of husbands
Illiterate	20	12
Literate to Class V (age 10 yrs.)	5	3
Class V to Class XII (age 17 yrs.)	10	13
Graduate	0	5

Note: Sakina and Kahinoor are illiterate; Manwara and Taslima are over Class V.

B. REPRODUCTION AND CHILDCARE

1. The onset of menstruation meant restrictions

Movement outside and friendship with males were restricted by parents as soon as their daughters started menstruating. Parents began to look for a suitable groom. One-third of the women surveyed had pre-menstrual marriages.

Table 17   Pre-menstrual marriage and age at first pregnancy

Wife's name	H.I. No.	Age in years of Marriage	1st pregnancy
Tita	1		13
Sabitri	9	10	14
Sherina	11		14
Sudha	12	12	14
Jayda	19	6	15
Renuka	26		15
Latifa	27		14
Rizia	29	'pre-menstrual'	
Chintarani	30		14
Sumitra	32	'pre-menstrual'	
Kahinoor	33	7	

2. Menstruation pollutes and humiliates girls and women

In olden days, the restrictions placed on women at this time might have been to ensure women rested and men left them alone. Nowadays, however, menstruation is associated with pollution. Women must not touch men, the granary or cooking pot, nor must they enter the cowshed, or these will all become polluted. Before women can lead a normal life again, women must bath and wash their hair.

Religious customs concerning purity clearly enforce and are probably at the root of these practices. Menstruating women are prohibited from entering the temple and mosque, from saying namaz and from going on religious fasts.

At an early age, although it is just an important part of the reproductive cycle, girls learn to regard menstruation as a curse. Suchitra (24) was kept in a dark room for nine days by her in-laws when she started to menstruate.

Everything connected with the female reproductive system except the birth of a baby boy, seems to be designed by the patriarchal system to humiliate the girl/woman and make her feel sinful and ashamed. Ignorance and shame cause a vicious circle where girls and women are extremely shy of and even loathe discussing any aspect of their reproductive life which then perpetuates the ignorance and shame.

Such values ingeniously ensure that men's inability to menstruate and procreate is not regarded as an inadequacy. Moreover, by making everyone believe that girls' and women's reproductive abilities are in fact their biological, social, cultural, religious and economic nemesis, female inferiority and male superiority are assured.

3. Women were married off against their will

Krisha (10) wanted to study beyond Class X and protested bitterly when her parents arranged her marriage. Her in-laws said they would let her study with them, 'but they never did.' Namita (20) had refused adamantly to get married, but had been forced by Biram's friends to return to the village and marry him. She had wanted to continue working for a family in Calcutta. Marrying off young girls before or as soon as they reach puberty is a denial of human rights. Although she may not protest and may even enjoy all the exciting attention temporarily, the child has in actuality been deprived of her childhood and the time needed to grow into womanhood. Forced early marriage ina patriarchal society may not only harm the girl's physical health, but it is also likely to have a devastating effect on her psychologically. Knowing that she will eventually have to go away and serve in another household for the rest of her life, she cares little for study or independence, and is thus moulded at an early age into docile material for domestic slavery.

4. Marriage brought further restrictions for women

The patriarch's need to know his paternal interest (whose father he is) led to:

a) Marriage of one man to one or more women. This ensured that all the offspring would be undoubtedly his, with everyone living in his household.
b) Prohibition of wives' contact with other men, thus preventing the chance of extra-marital pregnancy (and confusion of paternal identity.)
c) Covering of women's bodies to reduce their attractiveness to other men.
d) Extreme control of girls' and women's sexual life.

Observations of the married Hindu and Muslim women in North 24-Parganas confirmed each of the above characteristics of a patriarchal society. Tribal wives were similar to Hindus in dress and customs.

Thus:
a) In all households there was one husband married to one or more women. The wife and children bore the title of the husband. After marriage, Muslim women adopted the name Begum after their first name. Men did not change their name in any way after marriage. Except for Purnima (18), the women had left their natal village to join the husband's household which cut them off from their roots and weakened them socially (and, possibly, psychologically also.) The only two other exceptions were Chintarani and Kanak (30), who had crossed the Bangladesh border to start a newlife together, away from the mother-in-law who used to beat Chintarani. Also Sandhya and Ranjit (34) had been rejected by both their families because of their inter-communal marriage.
b) The wives surveyed were forbidden to go out of the neighbourhood and to talk to older and unknown men. Twenty women were utterly deprived, among them Firdozi (13) who said she wasnot even allowed to walk to the road running in front of the house. She said, 'My being unable to go out is like torture to me. It's even difficult to visit my sister.' Suchitra (24) was told by her husband not to talk 'so much', or her 'brain would shrink and life span

diminish.' Dipali (14), still young in comparison to her husband, has to defy the rules. She said, 'I do go out. I go to the cinema secretly when he's left the house, making a deal with Mamata to look after things. I do the same for her when she and Ananda go out. If I return after my husband and he asks me where I've been, I just tell him I went to the cinema and 'so what!' He makes a face but has to accept it. I can't manage if I don't go out occasionally. I'm sad, not because of the work, but because my husband doesn't let me go out.'

The freest women were the Tribals – Parbati (3), Gita (6), Sabitri (9) and Puspa (23). Women with liberal husbands were also less restricted – Rokeya (22), Chintarani (30) and Sandhya (34). Krishna (10) said she could go wherever she liked but lack of time and transport costs kept her at home. Purnima (18) lives on her father's property, but, though she can talk freely, is forbidden by Tapos to go to the market. 'If I die she can go. Not till then,' he said. Anima (21) and Reba (28) also said they could talk to anyone they wanted to but were not allowed to go to the market. Reba said, 'If women could buy things from the market, then there'd be no point in marrying. Why should he pay for my food, clothes and medicine if I'm so independent?'

Sandhya (16) has to carry food and clothes to and from her husband's work site, but he does not allow her to go to the market though she can freely talk to anyone in the neighbourhood. Sumitra (32) a Scheduled Caste fisherman's wife is allowed to sell fish in the locality, but is afraid to be seen doing so by her mother-in-law. Older women, especially those with married sons, attain a larger measure of freedom, like Saradini, Sudha, Jayda and Latifa. The lifelong poverty of Jayda (19) gave her a freedom to move about denied to women whose husbands and/or they themselves aspire to attain middle-class status. Having ensured his undisputed paternity and a free supply of domestic labour, the middle-class man can accumulate wealth and fortify the private possession of his woman by restricting her existence to the four walls of his house, thus ensuring his respect and honour in the patriarchal society.

c) The clothes of married women in the area surveyed served several purposes. The sari is cheap, covers the body from head to foot and restricts leg movement. It was compulsory wear for all the married women, though prior to marriage, girls wear frocks. All but a few wore the ghomta over the head in front of husband, male visitors and in-laws. The barqua was worn outside the household only by the wives of maulovi and not by other Muslim women, in this case illustrating how religious custom acts as the bastion of patriarchy.

The Hindu married woman's sindoor, which she herself re-applies daily, symbolizes that she is her husband's property. It also acts as a 'keep away' sign to other men. To distinguish them from Hindus, Muslim women are forbidden to wear sindoor or to paint red colour on their feet and Anwara (2), who enjoyed doing that, incurred the displeasure of her in-laws.

Without exception, Hindu wives in the area wore three bracelets for the benefit of the marriage and husband especially:
i) The white conch shell bracelet so that whatever she does will please everyone, and for her own good health.
ii) The red bracelet for her husband's welfare, so that no accident or illness may befall him.
iii) The iron bracelet to increase her husband's longevity, so that she may die before him.

5. Restrictions on older women are slightly relaxed

In the same way that older women, especially those with married sons, are freer than newly married women to move about and talk to people outside the precincts of the household, the clothes of older women (who have also lost their youthful attractiveness) may be less conservative. Aleya (31) and Sakina (33), for example, wore their sari without a blouse, and after breastfeeding their infants,would allow the cloth to hang so loosely that the breast would be exposed. However, this only happened when the husband was out, and there were no men around. As it was muddy on survey day, Sakina wore her sari up to her knees as she walked about the yard calling the chickens or with the utensils. On the other hand, her daughter-in-law wore a blouse with the sari cloth around both her shoulders and to the ground all the time, and when men were present, put the ghomta over her head.

6. Men are free

In striking contrast to women, neither Hindu nor Muslim nor Tribal men change their name or dress nor do they wear any symbolic adornment after marriage. Indeed, village men can go around with nothing on at all except a loin cloth, and nobody would bat an eyelid. Needless to say, both unmarried and married men are free to go wherever and to mix with whomsoever they like, andonly if a man's behaviour becomes particularly anti-social, will his parents start to criticize him. Ifhis wife says anything, he is at liberty to ignore her as he is at liberty to beat her and use her sexually. Anwara's father-in-law was such an unpleasant person that she and his son left to live at Anwara's parents' house (2). If a girl or woman makes friends with a young or middle-aged man, she will excite such gossip and disapproval that it would become difficult for her to remain unmarried in the village, as happened to the daughter of one of the Muslim women surveyed.Indeed, for this indiscretion, the mother herself did not feed her daughter for five days.

In a neighbouring village, a Muslim mother and her elder son made her daughter take poison because she had gone to the cinema with a boy. Yet, at Atghora, there is a well-to-do man who has paid money to enjoy the night with many poor girls and women. He has a bad reputation, but there are no restrictions on his movements. Dhiren (14) forbids his wife to go outside, and his daughterto go to the cinema with boys, yet he himself drinks regularly with friends outside.

Their powerlessness, and as their parents rarely accept them back, mean that married women have no alternative but to put up with unpleasant husbands. Similarly, there is no alternative for unmarried girls but to conform to the confined existence the patriarchal society would have them lead.

7. Mothers are much younger than fathers

Table 18

Average age of wives and husbands surveyed when first child was born

Mother	17 years 3 months
Father	29 years

8. Delivery of a baby pollutes

Men cannot bear children, so patriarchy evolved to guarantee the importance of the father and to ensure that everybody knew the paternity of each child born to the community. To achieve these ends, the role of the mother was degraded along with the status of girls and women in general. Their reproductive abilities were demeaned in order to illuminate the role of boys and men. Female dependence and control of female sexuality became the basis of male honour, fundamental to patriarchy and stability.

Sandhya (16) said she became 'unclean' after removing her own placenta, and that she would remain so 'until I bathe in the Ganges.' Suchitra (24) was not allowed to enter the temple or cowshed for one and a half months after the birth of a child. On one occasion, I was asked to cut the umbilical cord of a newly delivered baby opposite the house of Sandhya and Ranjit. There, in Sri Rampur, the rules are that the mother must remain in the same room where she delivered for one week. Neither she nor the room can be cleaned, nor is she allowed to go out into the sunlight.

Nourishing food is denied also. In Paschim Shimla village, I heard that pregnant women should not eat green leafy vegetables, and in three other villages, I met women who had been allowed to eat only fried potatoes for a week after their delivery. To blame these rules on superstition is to be only partly correct. The control of food allocation and consumption is fundamental to male supremacy in the villages of North 24-Parganas. The persistent belittling and weakening of women who are reproducing the society in a long drawn and very laborious process, is a deliberate and politically motivated tactic to weaken women and maintain the idea of male superiority in that very sphere where in reality, men are of much less importance than they would have everyone believe.

9. Pregnant and breastfeeding women did not get any extra food

Poverty was not the only reason for this because even wealthy households deprived reproducing women of nourishing and adequate food. Ignorance was not the only reason either, if indeed it was a reason at all. Everybody knew that eggs, milk, meat and fish are nourishing foods because these were specially prepared for guests or served as important items at weddings or given to the husband only if there was not enough for everyone. Thus, the particular diets prescribed by villagers for reproducing women or the total absence of any extra food in their diets would be largely due to their being reproducing women in a patriarchal society which has its own reasons for depriving and neglecting them.

Table 19   Women who got hardly any food

H.I. Nos.:   1, 2, 4, 5, 6, 7, 8, 10, 11, 12, 14, 15, 16,
        17, 18, 19, 20, 21, 26, 27, 29, 30, 31, 33, 34   Total: 25 women

Jeebanesa (5): 'I got so weak that I couldn't work properly for two months after delivery.'
Latifa (27): 'I got no food so to speak during pregnancy! Only once a day at noon and that

was only fried potatoes. People said that if the pregnant mother ate more, the child would suffer. I had tea at night. I got so hungry that I used to fall down.'

Aleya (31): 'After delivery, I have fried potatoes and ghee. I'm not allowed fish for five days. We don't give breast milk to our babies for three days after its birth.'

Table 20   Women who got extra food

H.I. Nos.   3, 9, 13, 22, 24, 25, 28, 32   Total: 9 women

Suchitra (24): I got oranges, apples, milk sweets and Horlicks during pregnancy...but ...after delivery for the first seven days, I was not given rice, porota or puffed rice, only fried potatoes. From the eighth day, I could eat vegetables, fish and only later could I use pepper and chillies in my food. I was not allowed to use kalo jeera. Eventually, when I started eating rice again, it was in the morning and at 4 p.m. only. No more. This was supposed to be good for the health of mother and child. I only had breast milk for a fortnight.'

10. Pregnant women served their husband and waited for them to eat first before they ate

Table 21   Women who served and waited

H.I. Nos.   1 (?), 2, 3, 4, 5, 6, 7, 10, 11, 12, 13, 14, 16, 17, 18, 19, 20, 21, 23, 25, 27, 29 (?), 30, 32, 33   Total: 26 women

Namita (20):   'He told me to eat but I would wait for him to return.'
Sufia (25):   'This is compulsory.'
Sumitra (32): 'My husband used to tell me to eat as soon as I had finished cooking, but is itpossible to eat before men?'

Table 22   Women who did not wait

H.I. Nos.   8, 9, 15, 22, 24, 26, 31, 34   Total: 8 women

Sabitri (9):   'My in-laws told me to eat early so I did.'
Sandhya (34): 'I never have to wait for him. Just eat when I'm hungry.'

11. Pregnant women were helped with the housework by other women

Generally, men maintain a boorish indifference to their wife's added burden, and rigidly retain the gender-based division of labour, possibly because they feel in no way involved in the reproductive process. On the other hand, women help one another frequently. There were some men who shared the work which means that all could if they tried.

Table 23   What help was available

	Number of households
From other women	17
From nobody	10
From husband	6
From other men	1

H.I. Nos. where nobody helped: 1, 5, 7, 8, 12, 14, 16, 18, 29, 33

Dipali (14):   'I didn't get a single day's rest before the deliveries. In fact, once, I removed the placenta myself and buried it in the earth.'
Latifa (27):   'After delivery, my mother washed the baby and cloths, but I washed my own clothesand cleaned the room after ten days had passed. My mother and sister did the housework.'
Reba (28):   'When I was in hospital my husband did the cooking. The second time, my motherhelped and my husband and his brother fetched the water.'
Chintarani (30):   'After delivery, my husband washed the clothes and room. He did the cooking for a fortnight.'
Sandhya (34):   'For about a week after the deliveries, my husband did everything.'

Note: Latifa's mother and sister would have come over to Latifa's husband's home to help.

12. Pregnant women got little, if any, rest

More than half the women surveyed had no rest at all during pregnancy right up to the day ofdelivery itself.

Table 24   Women who got no rest at all

Tita, Saradini, Jeebanesa, Halima, Sabitri, Sherina, Sudha, Dipali, Taslima, Sandhya, Purnima,Jayda, Namita, Rokeya, Puspa, Renuka, Latifa, Rizia, Chintarani, Aleya, Sandhya S.

Table 25	Women who got some rest.		
Sufia	5 months	Parbati	No cooking
Krishna	2 months	Reba	25 days in hospital
Anima	The last months	Sakina	The last 5 days
Anwara	No cooking for a month	Sumitra	The last 3 days
Firdozi	1 month	Jamuna	The last 3 days
Esmatara	1 month	Suchitra	
Gita	No cooking for a month	Manwara	

Total: 14 women

13. After childbirth mothers got little rest

The Census of India 1981 recorded that nearly 91% of rural women in West Bengal are 'non-workers.' All the women surveyed, however, had a very definite account of the amount of work they do and how much rest they get after childbirth, which is a type of work totally ignored by all government and most non-government evaluations or time and energy accounting processes.

Six women got no rest at all, nineteen got periods of rest varying from a few days to a few months. Jamuna (7) said that her parents would not allow her to return to her husband's household for awhile 'because they knew I would have to start working again.' When Tita (1) was pregnant, she was not allowed to return to her parents because her husband and in-laws needed her to work in their household. At the age of fifteen, she became pregnant for the third time, and after the delivery, lost consciousness and so could then 'rest' in hospital for nine days.

14. Babies of very young mothers died

Early marriage and pregnancy just after puberty resulted in the death of Jeebanesa's, Sherina's and Suchitra's first baby. There was severe trauma at childbirth for Tita and Sandhya Mandal.

15. Contraception is rare

In the area I surveyed where women are not allowed freedom of movement, it is very difficult to practise contraception. What I learnt about women's attitudes to this was from informal discussions only. Two women had a ligation after, in one case, giving birth to two boys and then a girl, and in the other, after one boy and one girl. The birth of boys is welcomed but not that of girls, mainly because 'a girl will have to be married off and that means a lot of money on her dowry which we poor people just can't afford.'

Krishna said she did not want another child after having a son. Those three women were Hindus. One Muslim, Aleya, carrying her eighth baby, said she had not wanted the pregnancy, but her husband had refused to allow her an abortion. One woman who had had a ligation was suffering from abdominal pains ever since, and the other had severe anaemia. None of the men had undergone a vasectomy.

16. Death of children due to sickness was common

In the area surveyed, gastro-intestinal disorders were a major cause of child mortality. Out of 35 women, 10 had lost children. Saradini lost five, Gita lost 4, Dipali and Aleya each lost three. Jeebanesa, Halima, Sherina, Taslima and Suchitra each lost one child. In at least three cases, lack of resistance to infection due to pre-maturity of birth which was in turn due to the very young age of the mother, may have been a cause of fatal illness in the child. Another cause would have been the underlying value-system of society which holds that women's life and labour can go to waste since these are not very valuable.

17. Childcare was done mainly by mothers and grandmothers (mothers-in-law)

Table 26   Range of time spent on childcare by wives and husbands

Range of time	Number of wives	Number of husbands
Up to 30 minutes	3	8
30 minutes to 1 hour	3	2
1 hour to 1 hour 30 minutes	4	1
1 hour 30 minutes to 2 hours	0	0
2 hours to 2 hours 30 minutes	3	0
2 hours 30 minutes to 3 hours	0	0
3 hours to 3 hours 30 minutes	2	0
3 hours 30 minutes to 4 hours	0	0
4 hours to 4 hours 30 minutes	0	0
Over 4 hours 30 minutes	1	0
	16	11

Note:
a) Where the wife surveyed had grandchildren, the time she spent caring for them is recorded in Table 26 and the time spent by others is recorded in Table 27.
b) Neighbours' children looked after children of surveyed households also, but the time was not recorded as it was minimal.

Table 27   Range of time spent on childcare by other females and males

Range of time	Number of females	Number of males
Up to 30 minutes	3	2
30 minutes to 1 hour	2	1
1 hour to 1 hour 30 minutes	1	0
1 hour 30 minutes to 2 hours	0	0
2 hours to 2 hours 30 minutes	1	0
	7	3

Table 28   Range of time spent on childcare by domestics (all female)

Range of time	Number of domestics
Up to 30 minutes	2
2 hours 30 minutes to 3 hours	1
	3

Table 29

Average time spent on childcare by wives, husbands, other females and males, and by domestic workers

Average time	Persons	Percentage of total average time
1 hour 52 minutes	Wives	37.9%
15 minutes	Husbands	5.1%
1 hour 26 minutes	Other females	29.2%
26 minutes	Other males	8.9%
56 minutes	Domestic workers	18.9%

Note:
Husbands' time includes 48 minutes to cycle son to doctor (5).
Other females' time includes 52 minutes to take grandson to doctor (1).

Men's involvement with childcare was generally limited to sitting the child on their lap or helping with studies. Sefa Uddin (22) was a notable exception. He spent even longer with his children than his wife, thus proving that men can mediate their physiological distance from the reproductive process in a conscious caring way.

'Dirty' work, like helping the child with toileting was always done by the mother. Anima said, 'Rinku's father doesn't help with that. It's mother's work.' Sumitra asked incredulously, 'Do men actually do these things?' Yet men can do these things. Ananda (chil14) took his daughter outside to urinate in the pre-dawn winter morning of the day I came to survey their household, and Kanak (30) used to do this for his children when they were small.

The work of cleaning soiled ground or nappies and washing the baby afterwards, was always doneby women – either the mother or an older sister. This kind of work did not appear to be done by older women and certainly not by males. Kartik told Tita to clean the baby's poo, and when it was suggested that he could do it since he was not doing anything else and his wife was cooking, he replied, 'Would women do men's work?'

This association of particular kinds of work with women, and the refusal of men to do it, indicates the strict and deep-rooted division of labour which binds women of all communities to the houseand children. Not only is this hierarchy rigidly enforced by each class, caste and community within the private sphere of the household, it is also fundamental to all hierarchy in the public world outside.

STATISTICS (Census of India 1981)

Maternal deaths: 1.2% of all rural deaths are due to pregnancy and childbirth.
Contraception: 85.3% of total of 3,980,224 were ligations on women.

Infant mortality rates:	Rural	Urban (per 1000 live births)
Girls	143	75
Boys	132	74

Sex ratio (Number of females to 1000 males): 911

SUBVERSION, FEMINISM AND AWARENESS

Subversion is a term which implies a steady organic breaking down from within and would be more appropriate for healthy and lasting social change than 'revolution' which implies a violent and bloody overthrow of one power by another. Since male power is oppressing females in a very real way in rural West Bengal and, given the complexities of a rural economy largely dependent on women's unpaid labour as the basis for wealth creation here and beyond to Calcutta, India and abroad, I have chosen the term subversion to describe a possible method of profound and lasting change. Subversion at the roots of each household and from within each locality would enable the evolution of harmonious rather than hierarchical economic and social relations from the grassrootsto the cities.

Given the realities of rural West Bengal, advocating that housework and childcare as well as outside activities be done by both men and women, would be to promote a subversive process. Certainly, many would consider this to be anti-social, irreligious, ridiculous or just impossible. After all, the social norm is that Bengali village men do not do housework or look after children, and that Bengali village women do not go out to earn money unless forced to by poverty. So to advocate the end ofthe existing sexual division of labour and its replacement by the sharing of all labour in the privateand public spheres by men and women and to try to actually change the norm in practice is to be subversive.

Feminism means different things to different people. It has often been misunderstood. The media has sometimes distorted feminism by showing television dramas where an educated rich woman is shown as selfish and lazy, causing endless problems for her hen-pecked husband and long-suffering father, whom she petulantly addresses as 'Daddy.' Or there is the America-returned Bengali 'memsaheb' mother, who teachers her innocent daughter how to dominate her husband. Such characters are invariably portrayed as ugly, cigarette-smoking, rich, miserly and vain. They may or may not wear trousers.

Perhaps a more truthful picture of a feminist would be of a person (woman or man) who does not accept male supremacy in the household or society and believes that female freedom is a pre-condition to freedom for everyone and a healthy society. Subversive feminism has achieved success in many places which may make some feel threatened which then provokes the productionof such exaggerated (terrifying or hilarious) characters in popular media, thus making the issues not just less threatening but also rendering women's oppression a non-issue that does not require analysis, debate or action.

To this end, the development of a feminist theory which can explain why and how patriarchy developed in the first place would be enormously useful. However, the reality of patriarchy means there are serious hindrances to the development of a holistic understanding of women's circumstances: those with the time to theorise, talk politics and participate in struggles are usually men, and men's reproductive consciousness and experience are different from women. Again, why would men critically analyse circumstances which give them privileges and which are not apparently problematic?

Much excellent research has been published describing in detail the characteristics of patriarchy in different localities of India and abroad. However, there is a serious deficiency in these empirical works. Even though many of these works have appended suggestions for the improvement of women's conditions, there is rarely any theoretical explanation for the why and how of patriarchy and little attempt to analyse its roots as the real need of males to define themselves and their roles in a reproducing living world as it moves from today to tomorrow.

It is inadequate to explain patriarchy by saying that men are physically stronger than women, or that male supremacy can be accounted for because women have babies and so stay at home. Matriarchies existed in the past and still do in parts of India, indicating that patriarchy is not natural, but only the result of a process of change over time. And, I would argue that such a process of change has been deliberately constructed and politically motivated to re-arrange the natural order. Nature and the reproduction of species pre-existed civilisation and the production of things. So how did they end up at the bottom of the system under the control of men?

Examination of monotheistic texts, legislation and cultural practices created during the evolution of patriarchies clearly reveals how nature and the female are demeaned, diminished and made to succumb to the control and needs of the male. Yet, at a fundamental level, like all unnatural man-made ways, the lengthy struggle to dominate women arose from a **psychological** need in men which could and can only be fulfilled at a psychological level. Therefore, a good theory has to explain the origins of this need at a psychological level in the spheres of:

1. The reproduction of children.
2. The production of basic necessities and accumulation.

Furthermore, the theory must offer a means of mediating alienation, being relevant to all and solving real life problems. In other words, such a theory should be subversive, regenerative, analytical, all-encompassing and healing in a holistic way.

1. In the sphere of reproduction, men and women's 'reproductive consciousness' (psychological experience) is completely different because their reproductive roles are physiologically completely different. Thus, men are conscious of loss of their contribution to the reproductive process, thesperm or 'seed.' The status of the man as a non-worker during the lengthy pregnancy of the woman, and the delivery of the baby by the woman independently of the man, mean that paternity and the value of the man's contribution to the reproduction of the species are eternally in doubt.

Thus, men devised ways to change matriarchal societies into patriarchal societies which ensure that paternity and man's contribution to the reproductive process are always recognised and honoured. And, because paternity and men's value in the process of reproduction could always be in doubt, patriarchal values and practices are applied ruthlessly. Over the centuries, boys and men have captured, enslaved, raped and murdered girls and women, and evolved cultures, religions, legislation, institutions, land tenure and family structures in order to establish their control over women and ensure male authority is unassailable; all in order to overcome their sense of loss, insecurity and inferiority in the sphere of reproduction. Many women too have supported and perpetrated male domination.

Simultaneously, men's role in reproduction has been idealised and given significance in mythological ways to compensate for the lack of real significance, and women's role has been denigrated. The natural world was also demeaned, as a study of ancient (including religious) texts will reveal. In recent times, a production system developed, based on slavery and the privatisation of social assets like land and money. Hierarchy, inequity and violence characterise societies where gender roles are hierarchical and inequitable; where men, believing their status, authority or 'mark' have not been adequately honoured and acknowledged, kill those who humiliate them and slaughter those they see as enemies – the practical application of a state of mind utterly alienated from the maternal.

On the other hand, men motivated by the creative instinct, though they cannot create life, can create things which are non-living. This process of creation is not only a potentially fulfilling experience in itself, but also leaves to posterity a valuable part of the creator. Men have invented and designed things of amazing beauty and intricacy, and composed art and music of intense spirituality that plumb the depths of human emotion, and though non-living, take on a kind of life which is enjoyed by many people for generations after the creators have died. The fount of such creativity is the urge to labour for a meaningful and spiritual experience which will leave a legacy, in a way, an experience and outcome similar to that of women reproducing a new life.

Idealising and deifying the Mother figure is another way men connect with the process of reproduction. In West Bengal, Hindus idealise the mother figure in the form of goddesses like the all-powerful Durga or many-armed Destroyer Kali. Catholics have Mary, the mother of Jesus whom they believe to be the son of God. There is an immense devotion for such mother figures, an extraordinary attachment that has nothing to do with real mothers' lives, but which, in its very idealism, may exist to fill some equally immense psychological vacuum. And the filling of this vacuum is so important for some that irrational concepts such as the 'virgin birth' and the week-long Creation of the world, are believed to be literal truth. Blind faith is a demand of patriarchs.

2. In the sphere of production outside the home, men have accumulated in ever-increasing amounts because, not being integrated into the reproductive process, they have needed to prove themselves in other ways. And it has been possible to accumulate on such a grand scale because as non-labourers in the private sphere, men can expropriate the free time provided by women, to become great creators and accumulators in the public sphere.

However, increased production per se will not help. Righting upside-down cultures that have evolved from men's need to prove themselves would, and this will only happen when men overcome their biological insignificance in the sphere of reproduction by supporting women during pregnancy and childbirth and by equally sharing the labour of housework and childcare.

REPRODUCTION (from sexual intercourse to the child)

Below I have given a brief description of the events in the reproductive process as they affect women and men physically and at the level of the consciousness.

For the female
1. Keeps the seeds of sexual intercourse. There is no sense of loss
2. During pregnancy, she nourishes new life within her own body. She is naturally integrated in the reproductive process
3. Delivery. She gives birth to her child.
4. She is creative naturally; integrated as a creator in history, today and the future. She does not need the public world of money, commodities, laws, or customs to sanction her maternity. There is no doubt that the child is hers since maternity is a lived and witnessed experience.
5. The child is valuable both because of the inherent worth of the mother's reproductive labour and because the baby has her/his own value as a new life.

For the male
1. He loses the seed of sexual intercourse. There is a sense of loss.
2. He does not nourish new life within himself and is, therefore, not naturally integrated in the reproductive process or in natural time.
3. He does not give birth and his presence is not essential.
4. Paternity is an ideal concept and, without effort, not a lived experience.
5. He attains self-respect, social status and worth by creating, producing and accumulating in the public world. But these are artificial, risky and often unnecessary processes.
6. To destroy doubt about paternity, patriarchal systems evolved: the male appropriates the value of both the mother and the child by making them bear his name and live in his home.

Male domination in society and the household is rooted in men's consciousness. This is the theory, and this theory is applied to interpret conditions in the area surveyed in North 24-Parganas. It will never be possible to remove the depravity that is male domination unless its roots are dug up and exposed for what they are – men's need to have significance in a society created by women.

The Means of Reproduction

Three basic issues are involved here:

1. The woman's authority over her own body

Bengali village women generally do not have complete and independent control over their own body.
a) The system of arranged/forced marriage, especially when the girl is still a child, is the chief violence used to deprive women of control over their own means of reproduction.

b) Women are often not allowed to practise contraception or to have an abortion. It is usually the wife who undergoes sterilisation; government and family pressurising her to have the operation rather than the husband, even though the vasectomy is a much less complicated and painful procedure.

c) If a girl is born, the mother may have to endure repeated pregnancies until a son is born. Decisions regarding whether she needs to become pregnant or not are often made by her husband or mother-in-law and not by her.

2. <u>Privileges due to the pregnant woman and breastfeeding mother</u>

Bengali village women rarely enjoy sufficient food, care or rest during pregnancy. Prevailing customs like waiting for the husband to finish his meal continue to be followed during the vital reproductive periods. Delivery is often undergone in unhygienic surroundings and pain and discomfort are compounded by anti-maternal customs such as denying the mother a bath, fresh air, sunshine and adequate food.

3. <u>The place of reproduction</u>

Bengali village women leave their parents and go to stay with the husband at his parents' home which is often very far from the natal home. This weakens women in the following ways:

a) From birth, a girl is generally regarded by her parents as an object for others (porer jinish.) Consequently, she is deprived and discriminated against. On the other hand, her brother will be expected to support his parents later, and is consequently given the best the household can afford in food, clothes, education and liberty.

b) The girl is taught that housework and childcare are the responsibilities of women. From an early age, her time and energy are spent on these tasks, while her brother remains free to play, to study and to work outside the home.

c) The mother of a boy expects to be relieved of domestic work after her son marries and brings home a wife. In this way, the lifelong expectations of the mother-in-law coupled with lack of education and involvement in the wider world, frequently result in bullying and abuse of the younger woman by the older. Bullying the vulnerable is always easier than challenging the powerful.

d) Often internalising the opinion that she is a 'thing for others', and knowing that when she is older she will have to leave her own home and serve others elsewhere for the rest of her life, a young girl may never be motivated to study even is she does go to school. If she appears too independent-minded, a girl can be severely criticised by her own family and others. So the ambition to become self-sufficient or financially responsible for others is not developed in young Bengali girls. The early expectations and training of boys are different.

MARRIAGE

Young village girls know that eventually they will have to leave their home, become some man's wife and spend the rest of her days serving him and his parents, bringing up her children in his household. Young, especially poor village girls have no choice in the matter, no freedom to decide whether to marry or not and usually not much choice about whom they marry either. Marriage is arranged, usually, 'forced', and carried out by the parents and families of both girl and boy, together with a holy man and witnesses. It is a family and a social event and life-changing for the two individuals, especially the girl who is a relatively passive participant throughout the ceremony. The Hindu process consists of rituals conducted in Sanskrit usually understood only by the Brahmin.

Women are taught that marriage, and early marriage, is necessary. 'Girls become old at twenty, so get them married off quickly' and 'The husband is the greatest teacher; the heavenly tree of a woman's life' are village sayings which seek to institutionalise and idealise the bondage of women. Women used to bear and bring up children in their natal home. Only later did it become customary for women to move to the man's house. 'Marriage by capture was an ancient form of securing a wife' and arranged marriages in rural West Bengal are only another form of this ancient 'capture.' The Hindu woman's mark of marriage, the red sindoor, represents the blood of the woman from the cut her abductor made on her forehead to brand her and also perhaps the blood of her wounded and killed relations. Certainly, the foundations of the sex-based division of labour in the patriarchal household are violent and bloody. In more recent times, having become institutionalised, marriage s a colourful, social and beguilingly mystical ceremony.

Marriage for men has brought many advantages, the two principal ones being:

1. An unpaid domestic worker who provides hard labour and various support and other services throughout the day and night. Since housework and childcare are considered natural work for women, men do not pay wives. Or, to put it another way, having captured the woman, the man can use her like a slave. It has been said that the first slaves were women.

2. A mother for his children who stays in his house for the sake of his self-respect and social prestige. Ever since man felt the need to establish his paternity, he evolved a system forcing women and children to stay with him and bear his name. The process began long ago. The spokesman for Hindu men, Manu, could not have compiled his Doctrines unless the views expressed were already held by a substantial section of powerful people who wanted the social practices pertaining to such views enshrined in law. For if women had not already come under the control of men by that time (possibly ten thousand years ago or earlier), it is unlikely they would have Manu's prescriptions to be followed. For example:

'Though of bad conduct or debauched, or even devoid of (good) qualities, a husband must always be worshipped like a god by a good wife.'
'In her childhood a girl should be under the will of her father; in her youth of her husband; her husband being dead, of her sons; a woman should never enjoy her own will.'

Women had already been captured for their labour and childbearing capacity, and now they had to be tamed and domesticated to suit the requirements of patriarchy. However, in Manu's time, unlike nowadays, men who wanted to accumulate riches and become renowned patriarchs, first had to try to please women.

'Therefore, women are ever to be honoured at ceremonies and festivals, with ornaments, clothes and food, by men who desire wealth.'

'For if the wife be not pleased, she cannot please her husband; from displeasure of the husband, again, progeny does not arise.'

Nowadays, however, the status of women has deteriorated so much that to be 'captured' women have to pay men. In Manu's time, marriage had to be made attractive to women. Now, village women consider themselves lucky if they are not harassed for dowry before marriage and deserted afterwards.

Similarly, Islamic law enforces practices which were being developed by patriarchs:

'When a girl is a minor it is permissible in Mohammedan Law that her father or grandfather or other paternal relations give her away.'

'The obligation of becoming faithful and obedient to her husband is imposed upon the wife.' A similar stricture existed in Christian marriage vows until recently.

The ancient form of marriage by capture gave way to marriage by purchase, 'and thus the notion of acquisition of a wife as property paved the way for marriage by consent subject to dower.'

According to Islamic legislation, 'Marriage brings about a relation between two persons of opposite sex, based on and arising from, a permanent contract for procreation and legalising of children.' One could ask what kind of a contract it would be when the terms are 'imposed' and 'permanent' for women; when only men have the legal right to 'talaq' but the wife cannot divorce herself from her husband without his consent.

Why have Hindu, Muslim and Tribal women been murdered by their own relations for marrying or even mixing with men of another community, though men are not punished? Do not all these laws prove only one thing – that men are psychologically insecure about their role in humanity's basic process – the reproductive one?

IMAGES OF VILLAGE WOMEN

The following proverbs were recorded by rural development activists from the People's Institute for Rural Action in the district of Howrah. Only a few have been cited out of the several hundred which were published.

'A girl is born in the family. O, what bad luck she has brought!'
'The birth of a girl is equal to a burden.'
'You, a girl, are born to eat up all the wealth of the parents.'
'A girl, or, a beast!'
'It is a curse of seven lives to be a father to a girl.'
'Kill the baby if it is a girl before she is a month old.'
'Son is wealth, daughter is waste.'
'Feed a son on a gold plate, the daughter on a banana leaf.'
'Women are like creepers – they live and thrive on men.'

The griha Lakhi image, where the wife is to be the goddess of wealth for the household, is one of the only positive images for Hindu Bengali village women, and as such, actually reinforces the family-oriented and housebound life of women who are supposed to be like Lakhi. The other positive, but equally restrictive image for women here, is as 'Ma' or the Mother. So under patriarchy, the Good Woman is the housewife and mother.

Marrying off your daughter is more important than educating her. Peasants mortgage or sell precious land – not to pay for their daughter's education and help her stand on her own feet – but to pay dowry to the future husband's family.

'Girls become old at twenty, so get them married off quickly.'
'Husband is the greatest teacher, the heavenly tree of a woman's life (which fulfils all her needs.)
'Man is a tamal tree whose right is to be loved; woman is the creeper begging.'
'A woman asks for life in order to be enjoyed by man.'
'Whatever a woman may do, later she'll have to become a slave.'
'Woman has no value, no respect without a husband.'
'Man has all the rights; woman, your all is at your husband's feet.'
'Boys will learn to read and write; girls will learn to cook.'
'If the husband dies, she'll become a widow; if the wife dies, he'll get another.'

Reinforcing the images of woman as an easily disposable object of no value and of man at liberty to do what he likes with her, are current village sayings like the following:

'If a woman is killed by her husband, she will find peace.'
'Killing a mongoose, bird or snake has the same punishment – just as for killing a woman.'
'If she tells people she's been raped, she'll be loathed by everyone.'
'Don't live with a man who doesn't beat you.'
'Woman, cattle and drums – the more you beat them, the better the sound.'

'The more you beat your wife, the greater pleasure your hand gets. Also, if you don't beat her, she'll be unhappy.'
'Torture by the husband is not torture at all; it is a declaration of love, oiled with shohag. Don't worry about it. The husband is god. Follow him always.'

Images and fantasies - the consciousness of fascist and fundamentalist patriarchs, women-haters, psychopaths, bullies, abusers and criminals – become reality all too frequently, but I shall not recount here the atrocities meted out on village women by their 'god.' Beating, psychological and verbal abuse, rape, desertion and murder of women by their husband, his parents and friends (at times with the connivance of political parties and police) are documented elsewhere, and feature as staple reports in the daily newspapers.

THE INVISIBLE REALITY OF WOMEN (India and West Bengal)

There is a vivid difference between patriarchal rural fantasies and the actuality of rural women's lives. The information given below comes from A) detailed time and energy use surveys of rural women and men within the household done by individuals and non-government organisations, and B) the Government of India Census of 1981 and National Sample Survey. Although the NSS has highlighted several domestic activities, these same activities remain unrecorded in the Census statistics. This 'invisibility' is itself a manifestation of patriarchal attitudes in educated and wealthy urbanites which replicate the attitudes of rural people, thus solidifying, irrespective of class, caste or creed, the all-pervasive control of women in India. Tables on pages 234 and 235 of the 1981 Census give details of the 'Working' population in the area surveyed – the West Bengal District of 24-Parganas (which, in 1981, had not yet been divided into North and South.)

A) The National Commission on Self Employed Women published the following in their report called 'Sramshakti': (See Bibliography for Mukherjee, Krishna-raj and Pandey.)

'There are a number of studies to show that women work for longer hours and contribute more than men in terms of total labour energy spent by the household members. On account of deeply entrenched social customs, taboos and prejudices, women's work continues to be invisible andconfined more to non-monetary activities. "It has been observed that the average hours of unpaid work done by married women outside the home varied from 6.13 to 7.53 hours per day, some of them working more than 10 hours each day. Apart from domestic duties, women engaged in agricultural operations work on an average about 12 hours on the farm and in taking care of cattle at home."

There are numerous activities like collection of fodder and fuel, maintaining of dairy, poultry and animals, vegetable growing, food processing, sewing, weaving etc. in which women are engaged and increase the 'household' command over necessities. The household would have to spend a lot of money in procuring these services if they were not rendered by women.

Women also supplement the household income often by taking on 'gainful employment' (the double burden), without the men in the household taking on any domestic work.

Other reports provide further information. In monetary terms, women's housework and childcare have been evaluated at about 50% of the Net Domestic Product of the Indian economy and 'Women spend 49 hours per week in domestic activities and only in roof repairs do men give a hand... The most time-consuming activity is fetching water, washing clothes and utensils – a task never done by males.' From another private study, 'The contribution made through household production to family welfare was as high as half of the household's income. This contribution which is primarily made by the housemaker needs all the recognition and must be brought into more visibility. The income accounting procedures should also be revised to include the real contribution made in household production to the nation's welfare.'

Finally, another extract from Sramshakti:

'The proportion of females engaged in domestic duties along with the free collection of goods (vegetables, roots, firewood, cattle food), sewing, tailoring, weaving for household use, is several times more than males. In rural areas, about 12.2% of female population over five years is engaged in these activities as against barely 0.6% in the case of males.'

B) The Census of India gives the opposite impression. Information on the numbers of men and women who 'work' in India was collected on the basis of the question:

'Worked at any time at all last year?'

Those who answered 'Yes' were put into the Workers category, while those who answered 'No' (mostly women) were put into the 'Non-workers' category.

The definition of 'work' was given as:

'...participation in any economically productive activity. Such participation may be physical or mental in nature. Work involves not only actual work but also effective supervision and direction of work.'

Unfortunately, this definition does not include the work of housework, childcare or pregnancy and the labour of childbirth, though as an improvement on 1981 data collection, the 1991 Census will record 'unpaid labour on farm or family enterprise.' However, even then, Indian women's endless backbreaking and unpaid labour will remain largely unrecorded. Could this be because Indian families' and society's wealth is so dependent on the enslavement of women that those with a stake in the system prefer to keep the facts hidden, and, when pressurised to try to collect information about women's work, claim that this would be 'impossible'?

In the introductory discussion to the 1981 Census, there is a remark which illustrates the general ignorance about women's contribution to India's assets. Perhaps the author is a man, for he writes:

'Non-workers constitute 62.45% of the population of India...In the case of females, <u>as one would expect,</u> the proportion of non-workers is quite high and for the country this is as high as 79.16%'. (My underlining.)

The Census claims that in West Bengal, rural female 'non-workers' are 90.62% and rural male 'non- workers' 48.59% of the total population. One can only speculate what would happen to everyone in rural West Bengal and India also if women actually became real non-workers for even one day! To say it is difficult to measure the value of tasks which are species reproducing and life-preserving makes one wonder how useful our accounting systems actually are, and feminists may well query the validity of philosophical, cultural and economic systems which do not give value to women's work in the household and as mothers.

Women are recorded as workers when they earn money (and there are many households dependent on women's income.) The 1981 Census indicates that both female and male work participation rates increased from the 1971 figure, giving women's participation rate at 5.9%, while men's is 48.97%. The NSS figures also record a much higher percentage of earning men to women. However, the NSS picture is more accurate because it also records domestic work participation: 66.13% women, 24% girls, 7.28% boys and 0% men.

What these statistics do not reveal are the reasons why fewer women than men are gainfully employed. Anyone conscious of rural reality, especially in West Bengal, would know that only a fraction of women earn money precisely because they are women in a patriarchal society. Thus:

1. Many women are not allowed out of the household.
2. In Muslim culture, it is often unacceptable for unrelated men and women to be in the same place.
3. Society considers that it is unrespectable for women to earn.
4. Girls and women are not educated or trained as much as boys and men, and so are less well qualified to work at certain jobs.
5. Women may be sexually harassed by employers.
6. Young girls are married off at an early age and thereafter become fully occupied with domestic and family work.
7. Since women do housework and childcare, men are free to go out and earn money.

The 5.97% of the female population who earn money also have the 'double burden' of housework and childcare if the men in their household do not share these.

Several committed individuals and organisations have been putting pressure on the government for the last two decades to have women's unpaid work accounted for in the National Census. However, they have been only partly successful: unpaid labour on the farm and family enterprise will be recorded in 1991, but not more than that. It is unlikely that such a sensitive and pro-female awareness will be able to influence the bastion of Indian male power, such as those who design the data collection forms, the bureaucrats and the politicians. What will appear in the national statistics is what the people in authority want to measure and record, and where people with money will invest their money will be where productivity can bring profits. The slavery of girls and women ensures that the tasks essential to maintaining home life are done 'for free', thus 'freeing' up the time and energy of men to go out and make money.

WOMEN'S 'DEVELOPMENT' AND 'PROGRESS'

Based on the false premise that women are non-workers, huge efforts are made to turn them into workers – to educate girls and women and to involve them in income-generating schemes. This is all very well, but, unless men are simultaneously involved in housework and childcare, all that happens is that women take on the 'double burden' or, when this is unacceptable or impossible, give up their studies or job.

It has long been known that girls and women are a deprived section of Indian society. Unfortunately, national, state and foreign funds are allocated to projects designed to, in a nutshell, integrate them into the flourishing patriarchal capitalist system, rather than to projects working to reduce the inequalities, ill-health, injustices and environmental degradation caused by this system. Income generation schemes for poor women have been started by both government and NGOs, and West Bengal's North 24-Parganas district has many such schemes. And, while individual womenhave benefited from the experience and income gained by participating in TRYCEM, IRDP and Oxfam programmes, a much more effective long-term strategy for improving girls' and women's status and circumstances would be if the same effort were put into integrating men into the daily grind of women's housework and childcare activities.

As things are at present (1990s), such investment goes largely into strengthening the system. Children's labour goes unpaid or cheap too. Well-heeled legislators make laws which forbid the employment of children, but the poverty caused by the system means that such legislation is ignored. Employers (usually, though not always male) benefit from the part-time, non-unionised and skilful work of children and women, and as the accountants' ledgers show an increase in 'gross domestic product', all the 'development' and 'progress' boxes get ticked. And, for the Marxists, my comment would be that all this would apply to socialism also.

SHARING OF HOUSEWORK AND CHILDCARE

Peace and happiness are political and spiritual issues, and, as such, are the wellspring of the work of political activists, members of political parties, social and community workers and people in government, legal, health and media-related careers as well as many others. Village panchayat members, staff of voluntary organisations, cadres of agricultural labourers' unions and district administrators all occupy positions of responsibility, leadership and power in the rural areas. They are political people in that they are influential and in that each has a consciousness of village problems and an ideology which guides them in the accomplishment of their respective programmes.

The struggle to be free of men's domination in the sphere of reproduction and the maintenance of life must be taken up by women and needs to be supported by all those who want to end the destructiveness and sickness of the present society. As such, all work should be guided by a profound consciousness of the problems of village girls and women – who are at the bottom of the hierarchy produced by the present system.

Apart from the material consequences of this system, there are definite psychological ones also. Absolved of housework and childcare tasks, and almost unaccountable to anyone, men have much more free time, energy and space than women, as well as much more wealth and power. Their working hours are limited, and cultural norms have erected protective barriers which enable men to escape from the unregulated daily and nightly grind women are expected to take on, just because they are female. Thus, an unfair system spoils many men, making them selfish and greedy. Cultural norms mean many mothers treat sons differently from daughters, spoiling the former and discriminating against the latter; teaching both from an early age how gender equals fate, inculcating the notions that what is unchangeable is all-powerful and also cruel, that negativity is right and a positive attitude is wrong and thus, over time, fear reigns over hope, superstition over science, fundamentalism over rationality, violence over peace and misery over happiness.

Cut off by the culture, circumstances and their own arrogance, from the world of the givers, carers and nurturers, men develop a superiority complex and start to claim sole authority to run society and interpret religion. And when the male reproductive consciousness of doubt regarding paternity is combined with freedom from domestic ties, (and, worse, selfishness and greed) men can move psychologically and physically from the private to the public sphere to become all-powerful money-makers and warmongers, hating women, dreading the thought of women's emancipation and enforcing, through patriarchal and unfair legislation, their superior status over women.

This enforced social superiority is perpetuated by another noisy myth to do with 'women's security' and 'honour.' Everyone should be secure and honoured – not just women. To emphasise women's personal requirements is to set them apart, to create a culture where women must stay inside and utterly relinquish any role in public – as happens when fundamentalist and fascist patriarchs are in power and when women themselves accept an inferior status. Such a set-up is useful for power-hungry men who need slaves for domestic work and young men to fight their wars, all of which results in violence, misery, poverty and destruction – the exact political opposite of peace and happiness.

Sadly, entrenched customs are unlikely to change soon. Astonishment, laughter, hostility, conflict and violence have been the responses of men and some women too, to women's assertion of independence and the suggestion that boys and men share housework and childcare. In rural West Bengal, those women who have struggled against patriarchal conditions, know what it means to suffer social ostracism and poverty, abandoned by husband and often their own family too.

Yet struggles have brought rewards too – hope and a taste of freedom unknown before. Furthermore, such women are actually living the change and therefore really bringing it about. Even one single individual's way of life has repercussions like a small stone causes ripples when it is thrown into a still pond. But individual women cannot change the hierarchical structure of society alone. Change comes when both men and women together, living autonomously and cooperatively both inside and outside the household, respect one another and share the work needed to live, be prosperous and reproduce the species.

AUSTERITY, CHARITY AND ACCUMULATION

'Sarvamedh yag karna' was a custom recounted in Vedic mythology that stems back some ten or more thousand years, where the owner of property would give everything away – cattle, utensils, clothes, food grains – in ritual thanksgiving on occasions of achievement or celebration. Sacrifice and offerings were exceedingly important practices of the ancients, reflecting their closeness to the natural world and the ease with which they could give away things. Possessiveness had not become an entrenched mind set and sharing as well as caring for natural abundance was very important. Individual austerity and simplicity in lifestyle and habits were the desired norm, and, possibly, the roots of this ancient way may lie in an even more ancient form of communism which would not allow private property or which simply did not know it.

The Koran makes it illegal for Muslims to make profit out of money, that is, to charge interest on money lent, and Muslims are supposed to give away excess wealth to the poor on a regular basis. The month-long abstinence from food and water during daylight hours known as Ramadan was based on a similar understanding that too much self-indulgence is harmful. The Bible records how the Jewish Jesus had a poor and lowly birth, and how later he angrily threw all the money-lenders and traders out of the synagogue. In their longing for unity with an all-pervading force, mystics of all religious persuasions subjected themselves to extreme abstinence and asceticism. The Buddhist concept of Nirvana is that liberation is only available to those who completely detach themselves from material things and immerse themselves in the spiritual. Today, there are still thousands of ascetics, and, while we might think that their lifestyle is extreme, it might benefit us to ask ourselves why sacrifice and austerity have been such important themes and practices throughout history, especially in regard to men's sense of freedom.

The roots of misogyny in the psychology of many religious men and their scriptures lie in their psychological and actual separateness from the reproductive processes which, instead of dealing with by involving themselves and sharing in, they have sought to distance themselves as much as possible from by taking the ancient practices of sacrifice and simplicity to extremes, ruthlessly avoiding any contact with women and developing patriarchal cultures where women and nature are inferior to men and heaven, and thus, subtly and progressively, replacing love with hate, courage with fear and compassion with cruelty. Patriarchs' gods control everything and are to be feared.

In the early 19th century, Dibendranath Thakur held a 'kalpataru' in Bengal (now Bangladesh) where he invited people to take away his possessions. Traditional Bengali men still refuse to give up the simple white dhoti for coloured synthetic clothes, and, even today, the respect felt for a person of 'simple living and high thinking' is a legacy of ancient wisdom. Dotted throughout India, there are ashrams where hundreds of poor people can get free meals. Sikh gurudwara provide free accommodation and food. The renowned hospitality of rural people who give away precious food and water to a stranger, is another example of an ancient custom of sharing, and there are many other practices which, to modern man, may seem mere myth or superstition, but which nevertheless remind us of an ancient wisdom – like the stories of floods and earthquakes which have been passed down over the generations, or the belief that a guest is a god. People do not easily abandon customs since these provide continuity with the past and a semblance of security in a rapidly changing world. Above all, the veneration felt for customs is almost instinctual; as though customs were like guides, about survival itself.

What is certain is that old customs of sharing are at odds with modern practices of accumulation, privatisation of common lands and public utilities, and enrichment of some individuals at the expense of others. Noteworthy is the fact that such modern ways have, without exception, been imposed violently, destroying much in the physical environment as well as communities and people's links with the past and often their language too; all this to facilitate the processes of accumulation and enrichment for powerful individuals – usually men compensating for their lack of involvement in reproduction. The colonisation of India via West Bengal by the British (English, Scottish and Irish men) would be an example.

What caused the development of acquisitive consciousness? Did it develop first in men when they realised that their sperm-seed was necessary for a woman to become pregnant? And, since paternity was doubtful, men felt they had to make women their possession and control her movements. What made men design spiritual, legal and cultural systems where women are held to be inferior and the woman must remain hidden away and kept as the private possession of the man? Why did sexual desire have to be made into something 'unholy' and damnable, managed by covering up women?

The origins, causes and development of human psychology and social customs are complex. And without honest discussion and analysis, the problems arising from the sex-based power structure and division of labour, inequity, hierarchies and poverty will remain unsolved.

LAND

Recently, the United Nations published a report which reveals the worldwide position of women in relation to their work and the process of accumulation:

'Two-thirds of the world's work is done by women. They earn one-tenth of the world's income and own one-hundredth of the world's property.'

Linked to the issue of men's need to control and accumulate because they are not integrated in reproductive processes, is the issue of land 'ownership' and the sanctification of land accumulation via legislation. Legislation and its enforcement have made the concept of land ownership a reality; a psychological need indulged by law enforcement. The modern practice of hiding the name of the landowner behind a list of traceless and faceless companies is the quiet way of controlling and accumulating land. Another way was to use weapons and kill off the inhabitants.

Patriarchal land tenure systems are instrumental in changing production relations between men, but leave gender relations unaffected. Where land is, by tradition, vested in women's and men's names, the introduction of cash cropping and capitalist agriculture results in a severe decrease in women's access to land and reduced food production for home consumption. Simultaneously, women's social status declines, their workload increases, and the processes generally culminate in the enrichment of individual men.

In India, Santhali tribal people have fought to prevent their lands from being plundered by outsiders. Their militant struggles have had some success, but, like Native Americans lost their lands to Europeans, Indian tribes have lost much land to caste Hindus, multinational corporations and the Indian state enforcing their control over the land and resources without the agreement of local people.

The daily problems of landless men in West Bengal call for urgent solutions. Designated 'breadwinners' by a patriarchal society which forbids women to earn money as wage labourers, men's inability to feed, clothe and educate their household members is felt particularly keenly. However, this is not the place to discuss the connection between land ownership, capital accumulation and the misery of agricultural and industrial workers without work, because these are only aspects of highly developed male domination in the spheres of reproduction and production, and not the root causes.

One of the main reasons of increasing poverty in South 24-Parganas where water is scarce, is the fragmentation of land tenure due to the patriarchal distribution system where the father divides his property amongst his sons and over the generations, small independent peasant farmers can no longer compete with large landowners and the Big Boys of multinational farming. Women remain as the dregs of this system, with no access to land at all. Yet it is the women who labour to reproduce and nurture the males of the families, who process the paddy, manage the housework, fetch the water and even give up meals so that the husband, sons and labourers can eat.

THE DREAM OF THE MARXISTS

Capitalists thrive on agricultural and industrial commodity production, the sale of goods to consumers, the making of profit and on the medium of exchange – money. Given the contemporary interpretation of socialism as a commodity production system controlled by the State, outcomes would be similar. Without access to land, forests or the sea to live off, people depend on money for their livelihood. Thus, even in a socialist system, if people cannot grow or catch their food, they remain 'wage slaves', or dependent on dividends from holding shares, or invest and gamble in the markets. Marx analysed production relations which exist outside the household and, for this reason, his analysis is inadequate.

Privately owned land, resources and assets may be subjected to more public accountability under socialism, but gender relations in the private sphere are not changed necessarily if the goal of wealth creation is prioritised over the goals of equitable resource sharing. And if profits are prioritised in an undemocratic state under one-party rule, a male-dominated and corrupt bureaucracy can develop, and, wherever leaders go unchallenged, megalomania and the army may not be far behind.

The Zenotdel was a countryside women's organisation in the Soviet Union which existed even before the Bolsheviks came to power. In 1929, it had motivated Muslim women to throw off their burqua and participate in an International Women's Day meeting in public. Afterwards, three hundred women were scalded to death and set upon by hungry dogs - such was the wrath of Muslim men. Yet, instead of encouraging such courageous acts by women, Stalin closed down all the branches of the Zenotdel a few years after he came to power, on the grounds that it was no longer necessary. Since then, women have been encouraged to work outside or go back inside the house again, according to the leaders' production plans; the double burden of work both inside and outside the home, clearly proving that the new system of production did nothing to alter the old system where men did not do housework and childcare. There are hardly any women in the Chinese Politburo which begs the question: What is it in the Marxist man-made production system and governance which is so weighted against the involvement and empowerment of women? And it is blind arrogance to describe as 'deviations' the cold-blooded murder of millions by Marxist leaders such as Lenin, Stalin, Mao Tse-tung, Pol Pot and others on the far Left who have treated people as badly as leaders, like Adolf Hitler on the far Right. Such mayhem and destruction are the logical consequences of male supremacy, where power corrupts and absolute power corrupts absolutely; the inherent fascism as the form of governance chosen by the all-powerful and supported by gender inequality in cultural and production systems and reproductive practices – the roots of which lie in such men's unresolved alienation from life-creation and preservation.

MEN ABUSE WOMEN'S BODIES

1. Marriage as capture - women's sexual slavery, sexual torture and rape within marriage.

2. 'Eve-teasing' - why not 'Adam teasing'?

3. Assault and rape - in the fields and streets

4. Prostitution - local and international 'flesh trade.'

5. Pornography - who finds what thrilling?

6. Debdasis - 'slaves of god'

Perhaps these main aspects of women's oppression in patriarchy would disappear if men involved themselves as much as possible in the reproductive process. Who would feel the need to dominate a process of which one is a part, and while humiliating and abusing another might give a brief boost to low self-esteem, why would anyone feel the need to hurt and plunder something with which one is intimately connected? Perhaps it is an attempt to feel integrated with the natural which drives some men with split psychologies to abuse women's bodies.

REPRODUCTIVE CONSCIOUSNESS

Men's biological inability to give birth to new life gave them a different reproductive consciousness from women and, over thousands of years, men have developed systems to compensate them for this and to enable them to control both reproductive and productive processes in the hope that they will feel fulfilled and significant. In the process, patriarchal cultures, religions and institutions have been established where women were made to appear inferior to men. Nature – water, land, sea and sky - too has been controlled and made, like women, to obey the will of men.

Overcoming this system requires a change to the state of mind which brought it about, and the best way to do this is for everyone to value the reproductive sphere over and above the productive one and for boys and men to become integrated in it by participating as closely as possible in the processes of pregnancy and birth, and sharing, with girls and women, the housework and childcare.

We must get our priorities right and we can start to do this by understanding this simple truth that, without babies and their safe and healthy development into childhood, youth and adulthood, there would be no human life on Earth at all. Nurturing life is what is most important, valuable and fulfilling, and a person's gender should not prevent them from doing it. Cultures and attitudes which discourage men from doing housework and childcare inevitably accept, if not actually promote, oppression, hierarchy and killing. It all starts with what is in the mind, with what one believes. For me, I agree with the fairy in the Arthurian legend who said: 'My kind know neither gods nor goddesses, but only the breast of our mother who is beneath our feet and above our heads, from whom we come and to whom we go when our time is ended. Therefore, we cherish life and weep to see it cast aside.'

EPILOGUE

In January 1986, I met Pramode, a Nepali Brahman. He and his wife were exceedingly proud of their little baby. Pramode told me he wouldn't even have minded being pregnant. He had been with his wife when she was in labour, encouraging her and trying to ease the pains. How excited they had both been at the baby's birth! Thereafter, Pramode and his wife would take it in turns to carry the baby. He would carry the baby for hours in front of him as he walked, slung in a bag across his belly, warm and comfortable. He would change the soiled nappies and clothes, bath, dress and cuddle the baby, as much as the mother did. Once he told me that he actually felt envious of her ability to breast-feed the infant and create a situation so endearing, peaceful and happy, a primordial sharing that is invaluable. Rare as men like Pramode are, his example does prove that it is possible for men to overcome their natural distance from the reproductive process by a conscious and love-inspired decision to share everything they can with the mothers. In this case, Pramode had to face much criticism from his own family, particularly his father and elder brother. But he would cheerfully tell them that they just didn't know what they were missing! This is exactly the point. Men just do not know what they are missing by not sharing housework and childcare with women. For, since that's actually where the action is, the fun and fulfilment are inevitable and endless. And sharing makes the tiring times easier. Instead of putting their intelligence and energy into perpetuating this anti-natural society which is impoverishing us, either materially or psychologically, and destroying our world, men should involve themselves meaningfully and creatively in the natural and life-promoting processes of which women are a part. By sharing the tasks of housework and childcare, men will rediscover their primordial humanity, this time, enriched by love, understanding and humility – the best first step towards achieving peace and happiness.

GLOSSARY

Ashram: a place of religious retreat

Balwadi: village crèche

Boti: blade inserted upright into a wooden block that rests on the ground

Burka - Muslim women's long enveloping garment

Dal – lentils

Dhoti - white cloth worn around legs by men

Ghar jamai – when the daughter's husband lives at his in-laws' house

Griha Lakhi - the woman who brings luck and prosperity to the family

Gurudwara - Sikh temple

Ghomta - veil drawn down over the head, face and chest of the Hindu woman

Jatra - play/performance

Jhal – spicy

Kolshi - water pot

Korai - large heavy iron bowl

Kalo jeera - black cumin

Lungi - cloth worn by men which is tied around the waist and falls to the knee or below

Ligation - when a knot is tied around the fallopian tubes to prevent pregnancy

Maulovi - Muslim religious leader

Namaz - Muslim prayer

Paan - betel plant, the leaves and nut of which are chewed

Panta - last night's rice which has fermented and is eaten for breakfast

Panchayat - village council

Purdah - screen to prevent Muslim women from being seen by men or strangers

Paisa - one-hundredth of an Indian rupee

Porota - fried chapati/flat bread

Porer jinish - an object/thing for others

Shohag - marital bliss

Sindoor - red mark applied to hair line on forehead by married Hindu women

Talaq - spoken to end the Muslim marriage

Tamal tree - Indian bay leaf tree

Tari - country liquor made from palm fruit

BIBLIOGRAPHY

Charles Everett Hamilton, 'Cry of the Thunderbird; the American Indian's Own Story'

Gerdur Steinphorsdottir interview with Troth Wells, 'Wives on Strike' in the Housework issue, New Internationalist, March 1988

Anil Agerwal, 'Domestic Air Pollution' – a report of a study done in Gujerat, published in 'Manushi' No.28

Luisella Goldschmidt Clermont, 'Unpaid Work in the Household' in 'Women, Work and Development' Series No.1 published by the International Labour Organisation, 1982

Mary O'Brien, 'Reproducing the World' Westview Press, 1989

Mary O'Brien, 'The Politics of Reproduction' Routledge & Kegan Paul, 1981

R.B. Sethi, 'Muslim Marriage and its Dissolution.'

Abanindranath Thakur, 'Banglar Brotakotha'

'The Ordinances of Manu' translated from Sanskrit by Arthur Coke Burnell

Carole Pateman, 'The Sexual Contract,' Polity Press, 1988

Aloka Kanra, 'Proverbs, Folk Tales and Women's Liberation' an article appearing in English translation in 'A Woman's World' published by Anneswan and the People's Institute for Rural Action

Aloka Kanra, 'Prachalita Probad O Nari Nirjatan' a Bengali article published in 'Bartaman' February 17th 1988

'Shramshakti' Report of the National Commission on Self-Employed Women and Women in the Informal Sector, Chairperson Ela Bhatt. Signed June 1988

Moni Mukherjee, 'Bread and Roses' published in the 'Journal of Income and Wealth' vol.8 No.2 July 1985

Maitrey Krishna-raj and Divya Pandey, 'Women Assist Change by not Changing Themselves' a Report of a study conducted in Sindhudurg, presented at the Fourth National Conference on Women's Studies at Andhra University in December 1988

Rajammal P. Devadas, G. Ramathilagam and S. Subasree, 'An Evaluation of the Contribution of Women in Household Work' and article about a time-use study done in South India, published in 'Women and Work in Indian Society' edited by T.M. Dak

Census of India 1981; Series 1 'Provisional Population Totals Workers and Non-Workers'

National Sample Survey 32nd Round, published in 1976 and cited by Devaki Jain and Malini Chand in 'Women's Work: Methodological Issues'

The National Campaign for the Right to Work

Richard Stites, 'Women in the Russian Revolution'

Marion Bradley, 'The Mists of Avalon'

THE BRUGES GROUP

The Bruges Group is an independent all-party think tank. Set up in 1989, its founding purpose was to resist the encroachments of the European Union on our democratic self-government. The Bruges Group spearheaded the intellectual battle to win a vote to leave the European Union and against the emergence of a centralised EU state. With personal freedom at its core, its formation was inspired by the speech of Margaret Thatcher in Bruges in September 1988 where the Prime Minister stated, "We have not successfully rolled back the frontiers of the State in Britain only to see them re-imposed at a European level."

We now face a more insidious and profound challenge to our liberties – the rising tide of intolerance. The Bruges Group challenges false and damaging orthodoxies that suppress debate and incite enmity. It will continue to direct Britain's role in the world, act as a voice for the Union, and promote our historic liberty, democracy, transparency, and rights. It spearheads the resistance to attacks on free speech and provides a voice for those who value our freedoms and way of life.

WHO WE ARE

Founder President:
The Rt Hon. The Baroness Thatcher of Kesteven LG, OM, FRS

Chairman:
Barry Legg

Director:
Robert Oulds MA, FRSA

Washington D.C. Representative:
John O'Sullivan CBE

Founder Chairman:
Lord Harris of High Cross

Former Chairmen:
Dr Brian Hindley, Dr Martin Holmes & Professor Kenneth Minogue

Academic Advisory Council:
Professor Tim Congdon
Dr Richard Howarth
Professor Patrick Minford
Andrew Roberts
Martin Howe, KC
John O'Sullivan, CBE

Sponsors and Patrons:
E P Gardner Dryden
Gilling-Smith
Lord Kalms
David Caldow
Andrew Cook
Lord Howard
Brian Kingham
Lord Pearson of Rannoch
Eddie Addison
Ian Butler
Thomas Griffin
Lord Young of Graffham
Michael Fisher
Oliver Marriott
Hon. Sir Rocco Forte
Michael Freeman
Richard E.L. Smith

MEETINGS

The Bruges Group holds regular high–profile public meetings, seminars, debates, and conferences. These enable influential speakers to contribute to the European debate. Speakers are selected purely by the contribution they can make to enhance the debate.

For further information about the Bruges Group, to attend our meetings, or join and receive our publications, please see the membership form at the end of this paper. Alternatively, you can visit our website www.brugesgroup.com or contact us at info@brugesgroup.com.

Contact us
For more information about the Bruges Group please contact:
Robert Oulds, Director
The Bruges Group, 246 Linen Hall, 162-168 Regent Street, London W1B 5TB
Tel: +44 (0)20 7287 4414 Email: info@brugesgroup.com

www.brugesgroup.com